OUTBACK ADVENTURES

Also by Matt Wright

The Outback Wrangler: True Tales of Crocs, Choppers and Shockers

OUTBACK ADVENTURES

TRUE TALES FROM THE TOP END AND BEYOND

MATT WRIGHT

with Kaia Wright

MICHAEL JOSEPH
an imprint of
PENGUIN BOOKS

MICHAEL JOSEPH

UK | USA | Canada | Ireland | Australia
India | New Zealand | South Africa | China

Penguin Books is part of the Penguin Random House group of companies whose addresses can be found at global.penguinrandomhouse.com.

Penguin Random House Australia

First published by Penguin Random House Australia Pty Ltd, 2018

Some of the names of people in this book have been changed to protect their privacy.

Every effort has been made to acknowledge and contact the copyright holders for permission to reproduce material contained in this book. Any copyright holders who have been inadvertently omitted from acknowledgements and credits should contact the publisher and omissions will be rectified in subsequent editions.

Cover design by Alex Ross © Penguin Random House Australia Pty Ltd
Typeset in 12/18 pt Sabon by Midland Typesetters, Australia
All photographs courtesy of Matt Wright
Printed and bound in Australia by Griffin Press, an accredited ISO AS/NZS 14001 Environmental Management Systems printer.

NATIONAL LIBRARY OF AUSTRALIA

A catalogue record for this book is available from the National Library of Australia

ISBN: 978 0 14379 711 1

penguin.com.au

FSC www.fsc.org
MIX
Paper from responsible sources
FSC® C009448

Contents

Introduction

I was raised in Papua New Guinea and the Australian outback, where living off the land and connecting with animals became second nature to me. From an early age I was drawn to animals most people would run from, and developed a love of deadly snakes, spiders and sharks in particular. My fascination for reptiles grew and grew, and I became obsessed not only with snakes but alligators and crocodiles too. By the time I turned 10, much to my mum's disgust, I had acquired my very own prized collection of one of Australia's deadliest animals, the king brown snake. I kept three of these beauties in a bucket that sat at the end of my bed while I slept. I'd take the snakes everywhere with me, and always seemed to be in trouble at home and school for sharing my 'pets' with my classmates and teachers. My mischief and love of wildlife developed as I grew into my teens, and if anything involved an adventure or rogue animal, I was there!

As a young adult, I was keen for my adventures to continue so I said yes to everything, upskilling myself and taking on whatever work was going. I've done plenty of jobs in my time – toilet cleaner, cattle station ringer, drill rig worker, Australian Army soldier, helicopter instructor and crocodile egg collector. Everything I learned along the way has helped develop my passion and skills for my career today as a helicopter pilot, wildlife conservationist and tourism operator.

For my work, I get to travel the world, capturing and relocating a diverse range of animals from crocodiles to wild buffalo and even polar bears. It's an honour to be able to interact so intimately with these animals, and I always have the preservation of wildlife front of mind. My focus is to remove and relocate problem animals rather than kill them, and I feel pretty bloody lucky to be where I am and to do what I do.

I love nothing more than sharing my slice of paradise in northern Australia with everyone else. My knowledge of helicopters, boats and airboats means that I've been able to create some awesome tourism experiences for people to come and spend a day in my life. But I'm not exactly a shrewd businessman, so there are some good-value 'What not to do' stories in this book about my troubles (and my successes) in setting up a new company.

I guess you could say that my lifestyle in Australia's Top End is pretty unique and it's something that the National Geographic Channel picked up on. In 2012, we premiered

Outback Wrangler, a TV show that follows my life in the Northern Territory, catching and relocating the biggest saltwater crocodiles in the world. Luckily for me, people enjoyed my story and watching the show, and we're now coming into its fourth season.

As you can imagine, there are a lot of hairy moments and touch-and-go encounters that come with my line of work. This book gives you a few of my most memorable 'outback adventures' over the years from Australia to Malaysia and the Congo. This dip-in dip-out selection of experiences complements my life story, which I told in my first book, *The Outback Wrangler*.

1
Two rascals

In 2004, our egg-collecting missions were pretty perilous. This was before the days of slings and rings, when we didn't have the luxury of a 100-foot line, harness and helmet to get us safely and conveniently onto a crocodile nest, so we had to use other means, which led to some shitty situations.

In areas where vegetation or uneven terrain prevents a helicopter from making a full skid landing, you've got to make a hover exit. And during egg collecting, this means jumping out of the chopper into the air, and often landing right next to a crocodile. Or, other times, getting dropped off as close as possible and walking my way through tall timber to get to a nest. Sometimes, as close as possible was a long way away. (The worst technique of them all was the provisional 'chain and stick' sling I invented, but I'll get to that later in the chapter.)

In the early days, it was just me and my good mate Jimmy who did the collecting. We were footloose and fancy-free and did whatever we had to do to get in and out of a nest without being chewed. We would pack ourselves but loved the adventure. Without the proper equipment and gear, overheating and exhaustion was commonplace.

One particular day on the Victoria River in the Northern Territory is ingrained in my memory forever. It was the peak of the wet season and the heat was unbearable – it was 42 degrees Celsius and the humidity was worse than a steam room. Jimmy was collecting from a patch of nests in open country and I got the gig of taking care of a creek bed that ran through thick jungle. It was my first time in this sort of setting and I didn't know what to expect. My boss had thrown me straight in the deep end with very little direction and I was too scared to speak up back then.

'All right, Matty, you go look now. Follow the water and don't get lost,' he said to me. And that was it. He landed his rattling R22 chopper at the top of an escarpment and I jumped out with my two blue banana crates and stick – crates to carry the eggs and a stick for defence. A radio would have been good but I wasn't going to ask for one.

I was fairly fit, so bouncing through the spinifex and rocky country into the valley was easy enough but the heat was pretty vicious, and not only was the sun burning from above but the rocks beneath my feet were so hot you could fry an egg on one. With every step, I could feel the warmth pulsating through the soles of my shoes. The heat was a good reminder to slow down and save energy, and it wasn't long until I got into the jungle.

It was cooler in there, under the canopy of trees, but while I'd lost the hot breeze I'd gained the humidity. And I'd been so focused on preparing myself for collecting the eggs along the river that I hadn't even thought about the challenges of doing it in the dense jungle. It was inhospitable. I struggled to move through it in a straight line; actually, I struggled to move much at all. I stepped one way and got hung up in vines, and stepped another way and got hooked on spikey bushes, retreating only to trip on fallen dead wood. I moved two steps forward, one step back and ten steps to the side to find myself where I'd began: on swampy ground and amongst razor-sharp grass.

I eventually got through a small opening. I stepped up onto a big log and jumped forwards into the air, only to drop right into a big spider web. Now, I can deal with crocs and snakes any day but spiders are not my favourite animals, and I had just managed to completely cocoon myself in this web with a golden orb-weaving spider the size of a dinner plate on my chest. I lost it, dropped my gear and started dancing around in circles, pulling the spider and sticky web off my body.

'Farrrrk!' I yelled, hearing it echo out.

I got the rest of the gunk off and stood back to look at what was left of the web. Its size was unbelievable: it would have been 10 by 10 metres, easy. It was thick with insects and even a couple of small finches were tangled up in there.

Spider webs are pretty remarkable creations. They say that if the threads of a spider web were as thick as rope, the web could stop a Boeing 747 aircraft. The sun peeped through the trees and shone down on the web, making it shimmer. Despite the big-arse spider, it was beautiful.

I grabbed my crates and stick, and kept moving. The path became easier to navigate and soon I found the creek. I trudged down the right bank of the creek through the jungle, looking out for a nest.

I was stopped in my tracks again when a golden tree snake fell at my feet. It made me jump a little but I kept walking. Then a few steps further, another three snakes tumbled out of the trees. One landed on my shoulder, so I put my crates down and picked up the long, thin snake, admiring its brilliant yellow colour. I was careful with it because their fangs carry poison – nothing fatal, but that was the last thing I needed. As I moved, they continued to fall like gumnuts and then slide off to safer ground. I must have startled them.

I checked my watch. I'd already been gone for 35 minutes and I hadn't even collected a nest. I'd spotted most of the nests from the air earlier, so I knew there were about six of them around. I could hear the chopper buzzing above me, assuring me that I wasn't alone.

And then I saw it. Sitting perfectly on the bank behind some small trees was a pile of scratched-up razor grass, sand and paperbark – my first nest.

Carefully approaching its vicinity, I kept an eye on the nest and an eye out for the croc.

'Where are you, girl, where are you?' I whispered.

You never know if the croc is hiding off to one side ready to ambush, so it's always a big relief when you can spot the croc before you set foot on the nest. I stepped carefully and got down low to look under the surrounding foliage, keeping one crate close, like a shield at the ready. In the other hand I held my stick firm, ready to jam into any unexpected teeth. My senses were heightened, tuning in to the slightest of movements. In moments like that, a pin dropping sounds like a hammer slamming.

I did one last scout of the area. The only place I could think she might be was the creek. The water was crystal clear and looked about six feet deep. A scaly tail poked out from underneath where I was standing. She must have been wedged in an underwater ledge. *Perfect*, I thought. Leaving her there, I quietly stepped back to the nest, keeping the crate in between the water and me. I opened the nest up, pulled out the eggs and marked them one by one with a tradie pencil. It was a great nest – I collected 50-odd eggs and there were only three infertile ones. When you pick up an egg you look for a thin white banding around its circumference, which tells you that the egg is fertile. If there is no band and the egg is a lighter colour, almost translucent, you know it's ruined. I finished packing the nest and kept trucking.

•

I already had one half-full crate, but it was still early days and the heat was getting worse. My light-blue shirt had turned a deep blue and my pants were wet with sweat. I hoped the chopper would fly over again so I could feel the cool down-draft from its blades. I stopped at a small pool and cupped my hands together in the water for a drink. The creek was idyllic, with delicate green ferns and sandstone rocks rippled with different colours of the earth. Minnows and a couple of barramundi darted around, an archer fish spurted water into the air to drown an insect, and a pair of turtles cruised along happily. It was a little oasis of life.

I collected the second, third and fourth nests without too much trouble, making sure I packed the crates with paper-bark and nesting material (not mud or sand) to keep them as light as possible. By this point, I had half a crate left to fill. Each time I arrived at a new nest, I would see the croc from the previous nest pass me by in the creek, heading towards the main waterway to look for a feed. It was like a domino effect of crocs, so I had to keep a keen eye out for more than just one.

By the time I got to the second-last nest I was all hot and bothered. On approach, I could see a 10-foot female sitting on top of the nest with her jaw open. *Phew* – at least I knew where she was. I put down my one full crate and moved towards the nest with my stick and the other, half-full crate. This time I was protecting the eggs as well – I needed to defend myself without destroying my cargo. As she came at me, I gave her my stick to chew on and, after a quick tussle, she spun around and took off into the stream. *That was easy*, I thought. I was having a good run, despite the heat.

I sat down on the nest with the crate in front of me and scratched it open.

All of a sudden an almighty commotion erupted behind me. It sounded like a T-Rex was thundering through the trees. I spun around and saw the gaping jaws of a 16-foot male crocodile lining me up. It was overwhelming, being sized up by this dinosaur of an animal and knowing I had nowhere to run to, but I had to make a move. I jammed the half-full crate of eggs into the croc's mouth and he slammed his jaws down, crushing the crate and tearing it out of my hands. He swung the crate around violently, knocking me in the chest and pushing me to the ground so I was belly-up in front of him. It all happened so quickly, but he was clearly more interested in getting to the water than munching on me because he bolted right over the top of me into the river. There I was, pushed into the mud with claw marks all over me and a torn shirt and ego. I got lucky. I climbed to my feet and took a minute to gather myself. I tried to salvage the crate and pick up any eggs that weren't destroyed in the chaos, but I was buggered and couldn't move properly. I was in shock.

The heat was making me delusional, I got vertigo each time I went from squatting to standing up. I couldn't remember ever feeling this hot, not even when I worked out bush on the drill rigs in blistering 45-degree heat. I sat back down on the ground to finish off the nest. I pulled out an egg and as I went to mark it, it exploded in my hand, squirting a milky green fluid. Some landed on my lip, making me gag; it was putrid. I grabbed a second egg and it popped again. The whole nest was rotten.

It must have gone underwater, I thought.

I was frustrated – I'd just lost some eggs in a battle to save my own arse and so I could collect from this nest and, after all that, the eggs were completely ruined. I had one crate full of eggs and another mangled crate with a few sad eggs. I felt a little defeated and didn't bother trying to salvage any more. I got to my feet and picked up the crates, staggering around. They weighed at least 30 kilos each. I had a fair way to go and they weren't getting any lighter. I just wanted to collapse, but I knew I had to find the croc at the last nest before I could rest.

I found the female croc straight away and she wasn't hard to move off. After a few pokes with the stick she bolted, but I couldn't get it together. My energy tank was empty. Carrying on and clearing out to the next spot seemed impossible. I took off my clothes, ripping another big hole in my shirt as it clung to my sweaty skin. I crawled on all fours along the bank, looking for somewhere out of the way to lie down. My body was tingling and I felt like I'd been hit over the head with a hammer. Then I started convulsing, and vomited everywhere. I rolled over into the shallow water and vomited again and again, and then completely lost control and shat myself. I lay there in my own shit and vomit, with stars spinning above me. I've seen dogs overheat and die before and I thought that was what was next for me. Even trying to cool down in the water was counterproductive because it was warm – and

I didn't want to go into one of the main pools because I would be croc food.

So I stayed on the bank in the shade and rested. I could hear other crocs as they slopped down past me in the stream. I just lay there silently with my crate and stick, waiting until my nausea subsided. Finally, I mustered enough energy to move to a clearing where the chopper could find me. To my relief, 30 minutes later it came and landed at the bottom of the creek. I hopped into the chopper with the crates on my lap.

'Jesus, mate, is that all you got?' my boss admonished me.

I shrugged. 'Yeah, sorry, mate. It was getting a bit hot out there.'

I was done for the day, that's for sure.

•

I suffered from heat stroke for three days after our Vic River expedition, so I was stuck in bed at the cattle station where Jimmy and I were living. I used that time to take it easy and brainstorm different ways of reducing the stress on our bodies while we were out collecting. I'd heard stories of some fellas slinging under a chopper and I liked the sound of it.

Jimmy came into my room that night and told me there had been torrential rain, and nests were going underwater on the Moyle. The Moyle River flows down near Peppimenarti, which is located about 300 km southwest of Darwin and is notorious for its big crocs.

'Big wet out there, Matty. It'll be a new challenge for us collecting tomorrow,' Jimmy said.

'Yeah, we'll be right. Hey, I've been thinking and I reckon we should try out a new technique. We should get a thick chain, like a pull-chain you use on a boat, with a big D-shackle on the end, and hook it underneath the chopper. Then we can put a plank of wood through the shackle and sit on the plank. That way, we can get slung under the chopper and dropped onto nests so we don't get as knackered walking in the heat. What do you reckon?' I asked Jimmy.

'Oh yeah, but things could go wrong pretty quickly doing that.' Jimmy wasn't exactly sold on the idea.

'Not if we only fly above land and never go higher than 10 or so feet. What's the worst that can happen – we fall and break an arm? I'd rather that than overheating and dying any day,' I said, convincingly.

Jimmy paused and gave it a few seconds of thought. 'Righto, let's give it a crack then.'

I am fully aware of how illegal and downright dangerous this technique is, and nowadays we would be in a bit of strife for doing something like that, and rightly so. Back then I was naïve, and collecting croc eggs was uncharted territory, so we made up our own rules.

We got going at first light. Jimmy and I flew the R44 to a clearing on the edge of the Moyle and we set up our base camp, where we would return to pack eggs and refuel. My boss went for a quick scout of the area in the R22 to see how many nests there were. He landed back and told us there were about 18. It was going to be a big day.

'Righto, Matty, want to give this harebrained idea of yours a go?' my boss asked me. I was excited to give this new plan a go so I wouldn't get so hot all the time, but nervous about the prospect of falling off mid-air and dropping down hard to the ground.

I pulled out the plank of wood and 20-foot-long chain from under the seat of the chopper. We hooked it up and off we went. My boss was flying the little R22 to save fuel, with me dangling on the chain beneath. These sorts of choppers are designed for a one-man band, not a two-man circus. Nevertheless, I was having a ball. I was sitting on the wood with the chain between my legs, holding onto the chain and my gear, while I skimmed along the top of the cane grass. We weren't trying to be silly, we were trying to be efficient. And it was quite literally a breeze – I was staying cool and I didn't have to face the jungle and risk suffering another heatstroke.

But at one point we moved from about 12 feet from the ground to 20 feet because of a patch of trees and the fear of god was put in me.

'Please never go that high again, that was no good,' I said to my boss when we landed. I realised in that moment slinging like this could in fact go pear-shaped pretty quickly.

•

We'd collected about 12 nests when we stopped for some tinned spam for lunch. We had a handful of nests left, but I still wasn't feeling 100 per cent after overheating on the Vic, so I decided to stay back for a bit. It was Jimmy's turn to sling in. From where I was standing, I could see the small opening in the grass where the next nest was located. Off Jimmy went on the plank.

He looked back at me with an 'Are you sure about this?' expression, and I yelled back, 'It's as safe as house, what could go wrong?!'

The water level was high, meaning collecting was much more dangerous because the crocs have full advantage. I could see the chopper buzzing around in circles and lowering down to let him off the chain. But each time the bottom of the chain emerged from the top of the cane grass, Jimmy was still attached to it.

'What the hell is taking him so long?' I said under my breath.

He lowered in again and then the uproar started – Jimmy screaming, 'Noooo! Stop!' He yo-yoed up. 'No, no, noooo! Please stop, please stop! I'm not going in, not this one!' I could just make out what he was saying through the noise of the chopper.

He was throwing a cracking tantrum at the top of his lungs. My boss couldn't hear him properly and dangled him back down; it was his fifth attempt by this point. I saw his figure rise up again, but this time Jimmy had dropped his stick and crate and was monkeying up the chain towards the chopper. It was hilarious to watch. My boss saw what he was doing and headed back to meet me in the clearing. He carefully lowered Jimmy to the ground and parked the chopper next to us. I'd never seen Jimmy so wound up – he was huffing and puffing, crying a little, and scarlet-red in the face.

It wasn't the right reaction, but I burst out laughing. 'Mate, breathe, calm down. What the hell went wrong?'

'Fuck that nest, Matty – that female is nuts.' He was shaking his head, pacing two steps one way then two steps back the other way. 'I came in the first time and the croc swung her tail at me and it clipped me, then each time she wouldn't go away, she just wanted to eat me, I swear! And when I saw the other dead shit around her nest I didn't fancy ending up the same way.'

'All right, come on, you're up,' my boss said to me. 'I'll lower you in and hover there for a moment so you can get a close look, and if you don't like what you see then I'll bring you back in.'

I turned to Jimmy who was still distressed. 'You wait here and drink up some water for now. But if I go in, I want you to come with me.' He nodded at me.

I got the plank of wood ready to slide into the D-shackle but noticed it had nearly worn in half. I found a piece of solid wood from a nearby tree – nothing old or rotten, I wanted hard green timber – and hacked off a decent log with my knife, slid it into the D-shackle and twitched it on with a bit of telecom rope.

As I got lowered down, I saw what the problem was and I could understand Jimmy's reaction. Everything was dead. There were about 30 chewed-up turtles, a half-eaten six-foot crocodile, and mangled fish everywhere. It smelt absolutely foul, and the nest was thick with maggots and bugs. It was a proper haven for a killer croc.

Holy hell, I don't want to come face to face with whatever has chewed all that shit, I thought. But I wasn't going to back off, because I'd just made fun of Jimmy and I was confident that with the two of us we'd be able to collect the nest. So I got dropped in and a few minutes later Jimmy joined me. We started collecting the eggs together, but I couldn't shake off a growing sense of dread. I had a bad feeling about this nest.

'I'll stand guard and you collect,' I said to Jimmy. I had my crate and two sticks in my hands, ready to go.

Jimmy was on edge, looking over his shoulder every five seconds or so. The worst thing about this nest was that it was surrounded by deep water where the croc could be hiding, ready to launch at any time.

And sure enough, out of nowhere she propelled herself onto the island, grabbing one of my sticks and thrashing around, tearing it to pieces. I hoped she would've given up then, but it was clear she wasn't going anywhere.

'Hurry up, let's get this done!' I yelled out.

She went at us again, lunging at Jimmy. I pulled him towards me, and we both fell in the water, gripping at the edge of the island bank. My heart was pounding and Jimmy was white in the face.

I still had the crate in my hand, so I fed it to her in the water and she grabbed a hold of it, scattering the eggs everywhere. We backed ourselves up onto the little island, right on top of the animal remains. I could feel the maggots wriggling around me. We scrambled to our feet and she came out with us. I fed her the second stick and she death-rolled, so I gave her another couple of good hits and pokes until she finally retreated. But I knew she wouldn't have gone far.

Jimmy hastily packed the crates with the eggs that weren't damaged and slung out first. I stayed back with the stick and a crate at the ready until the chopper came for me. As I landed in the clearing, just two feet from the ground, the plank I was sitting on snapped. Jimmy was already there, sitting on the ground, defeated.

'Well, I think we've established two things – we might give that nest a miss next time and we're not using a stick and chain again,' I said.

'Yeah, and we need to invest in a harness and make our slinging a bit safer,' Jimmy added.

•

It's crazy to think how far our slinging has come since then. We were extremely lucky that nothing ever went terribly wrong in the early days of collecting, given our cowboy approaches. Today, under the leadership of Mick Burns, we have developed equipment and techniques that have made slinging into crocodile nests a hell of a lot more secure.

We work closely with the Civil Aviation Safety Authority (CASA) and local Darwin engineers, and have designed the safest sling operation for external human load in the world. We now use a dual-hook set-up on the belly of an R44 helicopter, with two lines in use at all times, both equipped with manual release function and electric buttons that operate on separate circuits. The lines have lightning protection in the form of an electromagnetic shield wire, so the hooks won't release if lightning strikes. The hooks and lines are tested and replaced every 12 months, and we use harnesses that are certified to Australian safety standards, which are also replaced every 12 months. We wear a helmet, and carry a knife and emergency locating transmitter at all times. How's that for safety!

And when there are tricky nests on islands we surround ourselves with a big ring as a barricade. The ring is made up of shade-cloth material, which is wrapped around a series of metal rings. The ring sits surrounding you while you're on top of a nest and comes up about 1.5 metres high and has about the same diameter. It's more of a bluff for the croc rather than legitimate protection, but it does the trick most of the time and hangs off our harnesses as we fly through the sky from nest to nest. You couldn't pay me a million dollars to go back to using a stick and chain, never in my wildest dreams would I do that again.

2
Training the crew

It has always been a precarious task to train new crew in how to work safely with, and in close proximity to, dangerous animals. Whether it's someone making a cameo appearance on my TV show *Outback Wrangler*, a helicopter pilot or green cameraman, anyone getting close to wildlife must have an understanding of animal behaviour and how to act around them, especially under pressure.

People often ask me, 'How do I learn to work with crocodiles?' Or, 'What do I do if I come face to face with a croc?' It's mostly true that knowing what to do in those situations is instinctual, something that is innately built into a person, but a lot of it comes from experience and, like anything, heaps of practice. I've had crocs chew and smash up cameras and tail-whip people off their feet. I've seen camera crew thrown off horses, rolled by bulls and trampled by buffalo. When you're heading out bush for these jobs, everyone has to understand the dangers surrounding the work. Otherwise you can lose a man pretty quickly, which isn't something you want to happen.

In order to study a croc – or any animal, for that matter – you need to understand how the animal's physiology and anatomy works with its behaviour. Lots of external and internal factors prompt different reactions from an animal. For example, sounds, smells, territorial threats, weather and stuff going on inside the animal – like feelings of hunger and fear – all play a part. These elements will impact the way an animal responds to you, and the more time you spend with a particular species the more you realise that most of them act very similarly. However, it is a mistake to think that animals of a certain species will *always* act the same. That's an assumption, which leads to complacency, and complacency can lead to things going wrong very fast.

Another thing to keep in mind is how genes and the environment have interacted over time to inform the behaviour of an animal. Genes relate to evolutionary responses of previous populations, and the certain behaviour patterns they have undertaken to survive. So, with crocodiles, a species that's been around for over 250 million years, one thing's for sure: they know how to kill and survive. And this is something I never take for granted.

When I'm in a croc's territory I not only home in on the animal itself, but I assess everything around me. Situational awareness is critical. I scope out nearby trees as a potential barrier to hide behind, look for high ground so I can stand above the croc, and test the ground to see if it's wet, dry or slippery. I check all paths available to the croc and work out which route they are most likely to take if they try to escape. Nine times out of ten, a croc will take the track with the least resistance, which is the easiest for them to navigate. (Although this only applies to a croc who is out in the open and on the defensive. You would see something very different from a female croc who is on a nest and on the attack, in which case you need to throw anything you have – crate, stick or pole – into her mouth and hope she chews on that instead of you.)

The conditions in the outback are always unforgiving, so there is a real skill in consciously zoning out the foul stuff – the stifling heat, the swarms of mosquitos, the smell of rotten pig. They are all things that, if you pay them too much attention, will affect your focus.

This job has so many moving parts to learn about and be aware of that it's hard to know where to start when a newbie comes on board. I'm a big fan of baptism by fire (within reason) because it shows you if someone is cut out for the work or not. Although often, if a person is really inexperienced, you've got to go back to basics first.

In the early days, before I started filming *Outback Wrangler*, I had a job catching a few crocs out at Marrakai cattle station towards Corroboree in the Territory. A young Kiwi bloke by the name of Ross was working for me at the time. He was a great guy but had a lot to learn. He had come up from New Zealand and had no idea about crocs, so I had to train him in everything from the get-go. I eased him into it step by step. I started with small crocs, showing him how to work around them, taking it steady and not giving him too much to take on.

On one particular day, I was slinging in a handful of traps that we were using to catch and relocate some local problem crocs. I hooked them onto the chopper and flew them back to the Toyota land cruiser, where Ross was waiting with our boss, the station manager. The plan was for me to pick up the traps from the paddock then drop them off, one by one, to the Toyota. Once that was done I would pull each croc out of the trap with a head rope, tape them up and load them on the back of the Toyota, ready to be relocated. My boss was in a shitty mood that day; he was time-poor and was pushing Ross beyond his capabilities in order to get the job done as quickly as possible.

I was flying back with the second trap when I looked down and saw the first croc out of the trap. Ross was sitting on its back while my boss was pulling on the head rope, holding it tight while Ross gaffer-taped its snout shut.

This isn't a good look, Ross has never done this before, I thought.

It was only a six-foot-long croc, but the next trap had a big croc in it and I knew there was no way Ross could handle it.

'Leave the next one, guys,' I radioed down to them. 'I'll be done with everything in 10 minutes, so I'll come back and give you a hand with the rest. The croc I'm bringing in now is huge, so I need to do it. Just wait for me.'

I was worried. I knew Ross hadn't been trained in how to jump on the back of a croc. He was very impressionable, naïve, eager to please and well out of his depth: a bad combination around my reckless boss.

I repeated myself over the radio after I dropped the trap. 'See, fellas, this one's about 12 feet so please leave it until I'm back.'

I was flying over to the paddock for the next one when I heard my boss cry on the radio, 'Matt, Matt, Matt! Quick, come quickly, we're in trouble! Ross has been bitten, he's been bitten!'

'Oh shit! You idiots!' I flew back immediately but I didn't want to land too close in case the chopper spooked the crocs. As I came in I could see my boss holding the rope and Ross sitting on the croc, but not much else. I landed a couple of hundred metres away and ran over but was still confused about what was going on because when I got there, everything appeared to be calm. Ross was on top of the croc, the hessian was over the croc's eyes and my boss was pulling the rope tight.

'Matty, grab the tyre leavers from the Toyota!' my boss yelled.

I snatched them and ran up to the croc and finally saw what I was dealing with.

'Oh Jesus, you poor bastard.'

Ross was sitting there, white in the face, tears streaming down his cheeks, with his hands locked into place on either side of the croc's jaws. He had jumped on the back of the croc, thrown the hessian over the croc's eyes and misjudged. Both hands had overshot the eyes and slipped into the croc's mouth as it shut, engulfing and then crushing his fingers. He was stuck. And, knowing that crocs have jaws that can slam down at 3700 pounds per square inch of bite force, I could only imagine the pain he was in.

My boss and Ross were helpless. If my boss took the pressure off the rope, the croc would have death-rolled and torn off both of Ross's arms, so he had to stay put until I levered the croc's mouth open. I got in behind Ross and opened up its mouth, which stunk like no one's business and was festering with maggots from being in the trap with a rotten pig. A croc is like a snake, though; if you touch it under pressure, it restricts or clamps down even tighter. As I attempted to pry wide the jaws of the croc, poor Ross began wailing, letting out the most harrowing shriek. Finally, I managed to open its mouth enough for Ross to pull his fingers out.

'Get out of here,' I told him.

Ross sprang off the croc and I jumped on in his place, putting on the hessian in the right spot and taping the animal's snout shut. Then I got up and had a look at Ross's hands, and I kid you not, it looked as though every one of his fingers had fallen in between the croc's teeth. Sure, his fingers were crushed but there was not one puncture wound or any blood drawn. Still to this day, he is the luckiest bloke I've ever come across. Bitten by a croc without a mark, it was unbelievable.

I did my block at my boss then turned to Ross.

'If you're not comfortable doing something, you've got to speak up and say so! That was just plain stupid, and unfortunately, I can't afford to work with you anymore, mate – I'm sorry.'

Ross looked relieved, not upset, and I think he was quietly happy to get the hell out of there. To be honest, I think he was done with crocs altogether after that encounter.

•

I've moved a lot of people along over the years who haven't been the right fit for catching crocs, and many of them have included film crew. Being behind the lens is just as challenging as being in front of it, and you need someone who doesn't crack under pressure. The first person I trained for filming *Outback Wrangler* was my cameraman, Mark Priest. He was a fit, older bloke, very capable and a bit of a silver fox. He was one of the first people to go diving, snorkelling and filming with our world's great sharks. He's filmed broadnose sevengills feeding, a tiger shark killing and eating a grey reef shark, hundreds of spinner sharks in one place and up-close encounters with great white sharks, all captured outside of a cage. He was still alive to tell these tales when I came across him, so I figured he had to be all right.

The more time I spent with Mark the more I realised how special he was. Always looking for the next best adventure, his zest for life was contagious and the best bit was, he was egoless. His fascination for wildlife and the beauty in nature would make me stop to smell the roses more than I ever had. I took a lot of things for granted before Mark came along, but he reminded me of the simple beauty in the reflection of the sun on the water, or a unique marking on a croc. The passion he brought with him made me feel like I was doing everything again for the first time.

The first croc I had to relocate alongside Mark was a nine-foot female. The tricky bit was that she was in water. In order to get the footage, Mark had to partly submerge himself underwater without making big movements, which is virtually impossible if you're filming. If a croc sees movement in its periphery it will change its course immediately towards that direction. I've been in situations where I've been one metre away from a croc with a pig leg in my hand, and someone 10 metres away, off to its side, has moved, and the croc has gone straight towards the other person. They are incredibly reactive animals, so I made sure I spelt the basics out to Mark over and over again, just to be certain.

'Mate, if you see the croc swimming around don't move abruptly or do anything to disrupt her environment. If you leave her be then she doesn't have a reason to be aggressive,' I said. 'If she looks like she's moving in on you, that's a whole new story. You need to jump out of the water immediately.'

Mark nodded. 'Got it, Matty, all good.'

There really is a difference between a croc swimming in your direction and one coming to attack. If you don't give them a reason to attack, most of the time they are more focused on either swimming away from you or moving about their waterhole as usual. Mark and I moved onto the high ground above the waterhole, sussing out our location and chatting some more.

'Always be mindful to not muddy up the waterhole when you're wandering around it, otherwise we will have no idea where she is and then we'll be stuck,' I warned him.

'Yep, I'll tread lightly.'

It was a freshwater spring and the water came to above knee height, so we were still able to move quick enough and stay above water most of the time while keeping the croc in sight.

I moved into the water and turned to see Mark already kneeling down behind me, working out his angles. He wasn't anxious or uptight at all, he seemed very composed. I slowly waded through the water, making sure I didn't disturb the ground too much, turning over my shoulder every now and then to see how Mark was doing. It was only the two of us; we didn't have the luxury of a spotter or extra helping hands back then. I turned again to see that Mark had got right down on the bottom and was lying there. I stopped in my tracks and stood still. He was underwater for at least 30 seconds making absolutely no movement at all, aside from the odd small bubble. I watched as the croc swam right into Mark's view and imagined the epic footage he was capturing. Once the croc had swum a distance away, he slowly rose from the water, with no gasping or desperation for air. It was incredible.

'You've got good lungs, mate,' I said to him.

He smiled and gave me a thumbs up. As I approached the croc, who was lurking in the corner, Mark came in closer. I stepped out of the water and onto the bank so I had more height. Mark stopped stirring as I went to harpoon the croc. I locked onto it and Mark moved straight in on the action.

'Whoa! Back it off, back it off!' I said.

Mark had got a little too close for comfort and the croc's death roll almost smacked him as he launched in the air out of the way. He had focused too much on getting the shot that he forgot about his proximity to the croc, and boy, was he reminded of it quickly. I was holding the rope tight as the croc tired itself on the other end, swimming and rolling about. Mark cleaned off his lenses and got back in position.

'You've got to wait to move in on the croc until it has tired itself out,' I said. 'You usually give them about five or so minutes of death-rolling, then they calm down and that's your time to move in for the close-ups. If you go too soon you'll be cactus.'

'Righto.'

•

It was Mark's first mishap but he was definitely the man for the job. He learnt quickly and became more proficient as time went on. His only downside was being too eager. He liked to get up close to capture the perfect moment and sometimes I had to pull him up for getting a bit too intimate.

In the earlier days, I exposed Mark to three of the most dangerous crocodile encounters – a water relocation, catching an 18-foot monster and collecting croc eggs.

The croc relocation was a very close call for Mark and me. Catching a croc that size brings with it many added dangers. The most concerning is that it has the force to buckle and potentially open a steel trap and manoeuvre itself out. We had this big-arse panel trap, double the size of a normal one at about 10 by 10 metres and about three metres high. It was extremely sturdy, made of high-quality steel sheets from the local cattle yard and reinforced with narrower steel panelling just to be sure.

We'd caught the croc in the trap and it was hiding itself underwater. Half of the pen covered elevated dry land and the other half sloped down into the water, so I had a nice height advantage over the croc. I was inside the trap mucking around with the rope, trying to detach it from a pig leg then retie the rope as a noose. Mark was following me around, asking me questions and getting some stuff to camera. My mate Mick Jacobi was there too, standing on the railing outside of the trap, keeping an eye out.

'So now I'm going to use this rope to throw over the croc's snout and secure him,' I said to the camera. I picked up the pig leg. 'And I'll use this to entice him out of the wa–'

'Fucking move!' Mick yelled over the top of me.

I registered the horror on Mark's face as he stumbled backwards and I swung around to see the croc in mid-air, at least eight feet off the ground, flying towards us.

I instinctively chucked the leg in its gob as it landed at my feet. It bolted it down within seconds. I felt Mick behind me, tapping me on the shoulder. Any sudden movements and the croc would launch – Mick knew this all too well. He slowly picked up another leg and pole for defence. I reached my hands up, keeping my eyes on the croc, and Mick put them in my hands from behind. I was armed and ready. Mark stood in my shadow slightly to my left.

I had trapped us both in. I'm okay if it's just a croc and me in that sort of situation because I can work things out pretty quickly, but I had Mark to worry about and I could see out of the corner of my eye that he was still filming. For a cameraman, this sort of situation would send their adrenaline through the roof and a lot of people would flip out, but he jumped back, stayed calm and kept going.

'Don't move. Even if I move, I need you to stay dead still, Mark,' I instructed. I didn't need to say anything to Mick, he was sitting frozen at the top of the railing.

'Okay, I'm going to feed him this second pig leg and use the pole as backup. As soon as I chuck the leg, Mark, you need to scale that trap and get out.'

'Roger,' he said.

'Move!' Mick screamed again from above.

I darted to the right, jabbing the pole towards the croc for him to chew on. I fell onto Mark in the process and knocked him over, causing the camera to topple into the water. But he left it behind and scaled the railing in a flash while I chucked the second pig leg to the croc. It let go of the pole and snapped it up and boy, did I move quickly out of the trap. The croc launched again once I was on safer ground, spearing straight into the trap and bending it outwards.

'Back, back, back, both of you get back behind the car! This croc is nuts!' I yelled.

Mick and Mark sprinted towards the car. There was a large tree to the left of me, which I planned on climbing if the croc somehow managed to get out of the trap. It continued to launch itself repeatedly, ploughing the trap with unimaginable force.

'This is one crazy fucking crocodile,' I remarked.

It was no wonder the station owner needed it off his property, it would eat a person in a heartbeat. It hadn't stopped throwing itself against the trap, so I decided to leave it there overnight to give it time to calm down and so I could bring back some more manpower.

We caught and relocated the croc quite easily the next day and amazingly Mark was able to fish his camera out of the water and download the footage. I've still got the video on an old hard drive at home and it sends shivers down my spine. The footage turns to shit each time the croc makes an attack but you get a sense of how close we came to disaster that day. Mark did an amazing job keeping the camera rolling, but there are times like that where you have no other choice than to screw up the filming because it's a life or death situation.

Mark moved on to other gigs soon after that, paving the way for my current cameraman, Ash Dunn, to learn the ropes. Ash had been working on *Whale Wars* back in 2007 with the Discovery Channel. It was a reality show that followed the *Sea Shepherd*'s campaign against Japanese whaling off the coast of Antarctica. Ash was faced with life-threatening situations every day while capturing the *Sea Shepherd*'s attempts to disable the Japanese vessels and the relentless Japanese retaliations, which were often extremely violent. So he knew how to film under pressure. While Mark filmed a little bit of egg-collecting, it was Ash who got involved with filming in the thick of collecting season.

Training people and the crew in egg collecting takes even more work than relocating a croc. You've got to explain the basics of choppers, slinging, being on the nest and looking out for a croc. It is such a unique environment. You're in waist-deep water, and the croc is aggressive and always has the upper hand. It's not the time and place to be pushing the boundaries.

Ash joined me in the very early days of *Outback Wrangler* when I was trying to get a show of some sort off the ground. He shot a sizzle reel with me for Discovery, which is a promo that outlines the concept for a new TV show. Before we went out I took Ash and the rest of the crew over the safety aspects of slinging in and out of croc nests: how to check the rigging; hook and unhook; the communication signals; the line entries in and out of choppers. And when it came to the crocs, my only advice was: 'Stay close to me and listen to EXACTLY what I have to say.' I could have gone into more detail, but female crocs on nests are unpredictable at the best of times so I didn't want to plant one concrete idea about how to act because it's different every time.

I slung into the first nest and Ash followed me in. We were on a bit of high ground but there was water all around us. Ash is a strong, tall lad with big hooves, so he's a little heavy-footed. His footsteps shook the ground causing vibrations, which is an open invitation for a croc to come say hi.

I stopped in my tracks and turned to Ash. 'Before we go any further you've got to quieten down, mate. You need to step a lot lighter. I sound like I have a bloody elephant in tow.'

'Yeah, sure thing.'

We reached the outskirts of the nest and I helped him get into the right position to film me collecting the eggs. Then I got cracking and signalled him to back up a bit so he could get more perspective. But instead of slowly shuffling backwards, he crab-walked quickly, lost his footing, and fell into the water. It was no surprise that a female appeared instantly, within a metre of him.

For god's sake, I thought. Ash was lying in the shallow water with a 12-foot female at his feet. I was certain he was about to get his foot chomped on. It was really serious.

'Don't fucking move,' I said to him softly.

I stamped my foot repeatedly and managed to get the croc's attention. She came at me and I fed her my crate while Ash staggered to his feet and moved behind a nearby tree, panting profusely.

'This is no bullshit,' Ash said to me, as we returned to safer ground. 'I thought a lot of this stuff was half-staged but that was very fucking real.'

'Yup, there's no room for error out here.'

I called my mate Craig in, who was collecting a nest nearby. 'Okay we've got about 15 metres to walk until we get to the next nest, and Craig is going to get slung right onto it with us. Keep your wits about you because the chopper's noise means you won't be able to hear crocs approaching.'

'Gotcha.'

The line appeared with Craig on the end and he was lowered into the nest. Ash was standing beside me looking left, right, left, right, and rotating around on the spot making sure there were no more surprises. It was amusing to watch but I was happy to see that he at least had his guard up now.

Craig was coming down to land, about 10 feet from the ground, when a croc propelled herself out of a deep wallow and into the air, missing his foot by inches. She disappeared back into the water, but we knew she was still there and would soon have another crack. The chopper pilot didn't see the commotion, and kept lowering Craig.

'Ash, you have to stay here. Don't move,' I told him, then headed over to help Craig.

I got around to where Craig was but didn't realise that Ash had ignored my instructions and followed me to film. Craig landed in front of me and I heard a sudden scream from behind. I spun around and there was Ash on his back with the croc crunching down on his camera. I rammed her with my stick and she retreated, dropping the camera and leaving the crushed lens behind.

'My bad, Matt, sorry.'

'You can't do that, mate. I need to be in control of the situation as much as possible, I can't have you going rogue on me. The only thing I will say is, well done for giving her the camera, otherwise you'd be limbless.'

•

Not long after Ash's first run-in we had another calamity releasing a handful of crocs in a clear patch of water near a reef. It was a breathtaking day: the water was calm and pristine and a massive storm was brewing in the distance, creating a dramatic backdrop that was perfect for filming. Ash was knee-deep in water, lugging around an old-school underwater camera that weighed around 40 kilos, which is no walk in the park. He was squatting down in a channel about five metres in front of me, holding the camera half-in half-out of the water.

'Righto, Ash, I'm going to release this eight-footer right here and I'm going to walk up the channel behind it,' I told him. 'And you can get the shot as we come past you. She'll swim past you, but you know the drill: when she comes don't flinch, just keep the camera pointing forward and she'll swim into the shot. Keep absolutely still, otherwise she will have a crack.'

He nodded. 'Yeah, yeah, Matty. I got this, no worries at all.'

'Okay, here we go. Are you sure you're ready?'

'Yeah.'

'What did I say, Ash?'

'Don't move, you said don't move.'

'So what are you going to do?'

'Not move,' he confirmed.

'Okay, perfect. Here we go.'

I released the croc and walked behind her as planned. We were a metre out from Ash and . . . I couldn't believe it. He decided to move the camera to follow the crocodile. As soon as he tried to spin the camera, the croc launched out sideways and grabbed it, dragging it through the water, then letting go and swimming off. Ash just stood there, speechless.

'What happened?' I asked him.

'I was just trying to get the . . .'

'No, Ash, *what happened*?'

'I moved.'

'No shit you moved!' I was livid. 'You gotta listen to what I have to say, there's a reason for it!'

'Yeah, Matty, I get it, sorry. I'm not having a good start to things, am I?'

Ash was right. He got off to a bad start but 13 years later he has done his training, knows the drill inside out and has well and truly earnt his stripes. He listens a lot more these days, but most of the time he runs his own show and knows exactly what to do and not do.

We all get caught off guard. No matter how many times I tell the experienced boys to be careful around the croc's tail, they still get wiped off their feet. It happens to me too. Last year, I was acting blasé around a 14-foot male that I had tied up under a tree. I touched its tail and it exploded with everything it had. Its tail flipped me upside down six feet in the air, and I came crashing on my head with my legs vertical. It felt like I had snapped my neck. Luckily for me it didn't get caught on camera because I know the guys would have stitched me up and put it on the show.

•

I'm very lucky that I now have a very strong behind–the-scenes crew on *Outback Wrangler*, after years of people coming and going. I have a small team consisting of Ash, Jamie, Jez and Row who know the landscape, the local people and how to act. None of them are full of themselves and none have been chewed on.

One of the biggest challenges I had was trying to teach them general practical skills like how to open and close a gate, hook up a trailer, drive on a dirt road without rolling a motorcar, and station etiquette. Those little things go such a long way in the bush, and a lot of people have come out over the years who thought they were above being kind to people on the communities or above having to roll up their sleeves to get the job done. They didn't last long.

Then there's my on-camera crew for *Outback Wrangler*. Willow started with me when we were catching crocs on La Belle Station in 2011. He loved adventure and stuck by my side, venturing out with me, collecting eggs and learning the ropes. Because he's a bigger lad he's always had to be mindful that he's not as agile as the rest of us, but he does a good job of holding his own. Training Willow in the little things early on has helped hugely with filming nowadays because he knows all of the smaller skills and details that make a big difference. For example, spotlighting at night. You can't just shine a light and hope for the best, he knows that you've got to keep the torch level at eye line because it's at that level that you can see the reflection of the croc's eyes, otherwise you miss them. He knew how to drive a boat before *Outback Wrangler*, but I trained him in how to safely drive a boat in waters with a high population of crocs. Now he knows how to do it in stealth mode at the right speed and the right time.

My other main man is Jono. Like me, Jono has always had an innate sense of animals and adventure, so when he came up north to film from South Australia he didn't need much training. But he did learn a couple of things the hard way on his first day in the swamps. We had to relocate a 15-foot croc caught in a small channel. Because the croc was trapped, we had the advantage, and it was a good opportunity to train Jono in how to catch a big animal. I sat down with him to give him a rundown before we got into things.

'Okay, mate, when this croc launches out, his mouth is going to be open and he's going to head towards you, so you have to throw that rope as soon as he shows himself. When you get it over his mouth don't go pulling on the rope too hard because you'll get terrible rope burn.'

'Roger,' he said.

I was a bit worried that he hadn't asked me any questions, but nevertheless I had faith in him. He was wide-eyed and eager, preparing himself on the bank with utter concentration. He had never caught a croc before in his life but I knew he'd be able to handle himself.

I gave the croc a little nudge under the ribs with my stick and he launched out mouth-open, just as I'd predicted. Jono dropped the noose over the croc's snout as accurate as anything. His smile took up his whole face; he was loving every minute of it. His excitement took over and he pulled the rope as hard as he could.

The croc retaliated and pulled him into the water, jerking violently on the rope. Jono pulled back with his own force but then yelled out in pain. All of the skin on the palms of his hands and his fingers came off completely. He had to let go and I took over until we had the animal secured. It was the worst rope burn I've ever seen, it looked like he'd just put his hands on a BBQ hotplate. They were blistered and red raw. All it took was the croc to give one quick flick of its head and the rope ripped through Jono's hands like a knife cutting deep into butter. He was very sore after that, but it was a good learning curve for him and he learnt very quickly to resist the pull of a big croc, and to never grip the rope tightly. Even now, Jono watches other people and reminds them not to try to overpower a big crocodile. He knows to let the croc move around where it pleases, tiring itself out on its own accord. And it's only then, once it's exhausted, that you move in on it.

In this sort of work, if you're not trained properly or focused on the job you'll get hurt pretty quickly. It's quite simple at the end of the day: you just need to do what you know is the right thing to do. Don't exceed your training and conditions without instruction, and don't go along with peer pressure. There are a lot of times I've stuffed up good scenes because I've stopped addressing the camera mid-sentence to yell at someone who's in danger, but I wouldn't have it any other way because that caution and safety is why I have never been chewed or lost a man while out on the job.

3
The wild west

As the leader of the team tasked with biggest croc capture in the world, I had an enormous job on my hands. Within the space of two short days, me and my team of six had to catch 50 saltwater crocodiles and relocate them across Australian state borders. And these weren't your average-sized crocodiles: they all ranged from 12 to 17 feet long. In fact, five of them came in around the 17-foot mark, making them some of the largest in Australia. About 30 of them were males and the rest were large females. They were big and had even bigger personalities to go with them.

The Wyndham Crocodile Farm and tourism site in WA was set up in the late eighties and was a popular tourist attraction for more than two decades. It fell on hard times in 2012 and had to close its doors two years later, leading to the most remarkable bulk sell-off of crocodiles in Australian history. The farm's animals were also some of the oldest crocodiles ever held in captivity, so the owner wanted to avoid destroying them at all costs and was keen to see them moved on to another Australian reptile park or farm.

That's where, Mick Burns, the owner of NT Crocodile Park and local tourist attraction Crocosaurus Cove came into the picture. Mick bought the crocs off the owners, and contracted me to help move the 50 crocs over 900 kilometres from Wyndham in Western Australia to Darwin in the Northern Territory. I was aware of the farm's notorious reputation for having troublesome crocs who had been exiled from their communities for causing problems and unrest. Two of the culprits went by the names of Oombi and Devil. Oombi was named after Oombulgurri, an Aboriginal community where he left his mark after eating more than 25 dogs before he was captured and sent to the farm. Devil built his reputation once he was in the farm by breaking out of his pen to mate with a nearby female and eating one of his penmates in the process.

Willow, as always, was the logistics man for this job, organising the excavators, trailers, trucks, slings and other machinery and equipment. Mick arranged the special permits, which allowed us to transport the crocs across borders from WA to the NT, and as soon as that was sorted, we were ready to boot. Willow and Craig hit the road and I flew over to Wyndham with Jono and Mick. From Darwin, we tracked over the spectacular salt flats of Port Keats down through the start of Kimberley country, where the mouths of the Fitzmaurice and Victoria rivers meet, then over the scattered boab trees and rocky outcrops of Kununurra, finally landing at the croc farm in Wyndham. We met up with the last additions to the team: my mates, father and son combo Nick and Seb Robinson. But before we got started, I had one thing to discuss with everyone.

'Okay, fellas, we had slim pickings for accommodation so we're being put up at the old Wyndham hospital,' I said. 'It's not the most inviting spot but we'll make do.'

Mick had organised the hospital accommodation with Paul, the owner of the croc farm, who had left the hospital lights on for us, as well as some instructions for us to navigate the joint.

We arrived on dark at this historical-looking hospital. Some of the lights were already turned on, and cobwebs creeped all over the ceilings. I followed the instructions to get to our rooms.

'Ya kidding. We're actually sleeping on the old hospital beds?' Seb asked.

'It looks that way,' I said.

The door opened and Willow and Craig came walking in.

'I think I'd rather camp out in the swamps than here. This place is spooky as,' Willow said. Everyone looked like they were thinking the same thing.

I lay back on the bed to test it out and it collapsed inwards. 'It's going to be an interesting night's sleep, that's for sure. Let's hit the sack, fellas.'

I slept a total of two hours that night, and that's being generous. It was hands-down the worst sleep I've ever had. There was a constant creaking from a door swinging on its hinges, the tin roof clanged in the wind, the windows rattled, and it sounded like there was nonstop activity down the corridors. I could hear every one of the lads tossing and turning; no one was resting easy.

I rolled over and checked my watch. It was 2 a.m.

Jono, who was next to me, must have heard me. 'This place is deadset haunted, mate,' he whispered.

Then Craig chimed in: 'I can hear footsteps every 10 or so minutes.'

'No shit!' Willow called out.

'God knows what the other noises are, but this place is the absolute pits,' Seb said.

'Why are you scared, Sebby? You're sleeping with your dad!' I yelled across the room.

The room burst out laughing. Everyone was wide awake and equally disturbed by the place. But I was a little concerned that no one was getting any sleep the night before the biggest relocation of our lives.

'We've got four hours left of shut-eye, so let's make the most of it,' I told them. 'Shove ya pillow over your eyes, count sheep or do whatever works to get some rest. I'll find us somewhere else for tomorrow night.'

•

It was game on at 6 a.m., and time to catch those monster crocs. We'd brought along a road train with three trailers on the back, which we typically used to cart wild bulls. These were going to be our means of transport for the crocs. We rolled massive hay bales out onto the bases of the trailers to make it more comfortable for the crocodiles, and then we were ready for the real work.

The owner of the farm, Paul, guided the way. 'We'll start with this pen here, lads. The biggest croc we have at the farm is in this pen, but he's in there by himself and he's also the most placid so it's probably a good one to warm up with.'

'Roger. How big?' I asked.

'Just over 17 feet and weighing in at almost a tonne.'

'Is the croc you're talking about called Axel?' Nick asked.

'Yeah, mate, have you heard the stories about him?'

'Yeah, they're pretty outrageous, tell the rest of the lads,' Nick said.

'Well, before my time, one of the old workers at the croc farm used to stick his seven-year-old daughter on the back of Axel and he would just sit there without a worry in the world.'

'Ya kidding? That's just plain stupid,' I commented.

'Yeah, pretty nuts,' Paul agreed. 'But I guess it illustrates just how docile this big fella is.'

I couldn't believe what I'd heard. I don't care how docile a croc is, it's still an apex predator and anything can happen. 'Fellas, don't go into this pen with your guard down, okay?'

Everyone heard me. 'Righto.'

I went in alone to start with, stick in hand. Axel was out of the water and sitting on a concrete slab. I poked him . . . nothing. I poked him again . . . still nothing. He just sat there like a statue. I half-questioned whether the thing was even alive. I went over and crouched alongside him. He opened his jaws a bit, confirming he was still in the land of the living, but there were no big movements. It was crazy, I'd never seen anything like it.

'Jesus, lads, I don't know if I want to give this animal the drugs. It's like he's already had them!' I walked towards his tail and administered a sedative, which relaxes the croc's muscles. I gave him a small dose, just to be safe, before we attempted to move him. After 20 minutes, we picked him up and put him straight on the forklift and into the truck parked in the shade. I hadn't even needed a head rope, harpoon or stick for defence. He was as placid as anything.

We had more machinery than we knew what to do with – forklifts of all sizes, telehandlers, a range of excavators, a front-end loader, motor vehicles, a road train, choppers, ropes and slings for days. And enough men to run a cattle station, because we weren't there just to catch and move the crocs, we also had to knock down the infrastructure at the farm to ensure we had enough space to move around in. There were fences, steps, railings and massive concrete walls to get rid of. It was like a demolition party with some prehistoric monsters involved too – a bloke's perfect idea of fun, really.

I was excited by the adventure to come, but I was also very saddened by the whole operation. So much history was being lost because of the WA government's uninformed policy on collecting crocodile eggs from the wild. The policy only allowed the farm to collect 500 eggs a year, which sent them broke. It was sad to see a local business shut down and a good tourism attraction lost.

Axel's pen was right next to the road train, so he was an easy move. But before we touched any more crocs we had to knock down some of the main walls. Willow got going on an excavator, pulling out the concrete that surrounded the premises. We nickname Willow 'The Operator', and for good reason.

Once the big stuff was done it was time to target the remaining individual pens. Paul told us that on average there were about four to five crocs in each pen, and every pen had at least one territorial male that was totally nuts. And a few of the larger, more aggressive crocs had a pen to themselves.

We separated into small groups of two and three and got cracking, starting from the pen that was furthest away and working our way back towards the truck. A couple of the farm workers went around before we got to our pens, partially draining out the water with a fire pump to make our jobs a little easier. Mick and I paired up, and Paul worked his way around the groups letting everyone know what to expect in each pen.

'Okay, this one is a pen with a single male, about 15 feet long,' Paul said, when he reached Mick and me.

We opened the door and quietly snuck in, with our crates and sticks in tow. The rotting smell from the patch of dark muddy water saturated the air. As I shut the door behind me I saw a sign a sign saying BEWARE OF THE DEVIL.

'Ah, shit,' I said. 'Here we go, Mick, we're just about to meet the infamous Devil. Strap yourself in.'

'Of course we're the ones who get this guy,' Mick said, sarcastically. 'Here's an idea, mate – Craig and Jono are next to us, we'll tell them this one is really placid and I'll rip the sign down, then we'll move onto the next one and leave them to it,' he continued, with a big smirk plastered across his face.

We both cracked up laughing – 'If only we were that mean!' – and then we stopped talking shit and got into it. Tiptoeing about, we sussed out our surroundings. It was only a small pen, so there wasn't much room.

We stepped cautiously down to the water's edge and, without warning, the croc sprang out from the water, making straight for Mick. Mick hurled his crate at him and the croc wasn't impressed, chomping down a couple of times and spitting it straight out. I chucked my crate as backup, but he didn't have a real go at that either.

I wasn't in the right position to help, so it was up to Mick and his stick to fend him off. Mick spun back to the croc but because the water had just been pumped out of the pen, the wet concrete surface was like a slippery slide. In what seemed like slow motion, Mick's stick went into the croc's mouth, then, still holding onto the stick, Mick slid three metres to the right of the crocodile, half pushing the animal back into the water. But as he slid down around to the croc's side, he lost grip of the stick and landed in the shallow water, on top of the croc's tail.

'Fuck, Mick!' I yelled.

I was at the croc's snout, so I poked and prodded it like mad, drawing the attention away from Mick, who was scrambling to his feet. Mick ran up behind me and Devil retreated into what was left of his water.

I turned to Mick, who was covered in the tar-like black mud. The smell coming off him was unbearable, which was no surprise because the muddy water was laden with old faeces and dead shit that had been decomposing and fermenting for years. It's hard to explain unless you've been around dead things before, but think of the worst stench you've ever experienced, then times that by 10. And a decomposed animal is the worst of them all. As a carcass breaks down in the heat, it begins to bloat up and smell, and then as it starts to decay, it deflates right down like a melted candle. The fluids and fat just melt out, spreading everywhere. That's what the mud was made up of and that's what was all over Mick. I was gagging, and Mick was gagging at his own stench.

We exited the pen and ran straight to the pressure hose, where I sprayed him down immediately. We were well aware of the risks associated with working in the mud. It was about more than just washing away the smell – the mud was disease-ridden. The crocs were one danger, but equally as life-threatening was a disease called melioidosis (more commonly known as Nightcliff Gardeners Disease). The disease can be fatal and is found in tropical areas throughout the world, particularly in northern Australia. The bacteria that causes the disease enters your body through small cuts or can be transmitted from breathing in contaminated air. In endemic areas, like the Kimberley region, people are warned to avoid contact with soil, mud and surface water. When we'd moved Axel out of his pen earlier that day we'd all been walking on eggshells trying to avoid contact with the muddy water, and now here was Mick covered head to toe in it. The farm was a haven for crocs, not humans. I made sure Mick was thoroughly hosed off before we returned for round two with our cranky mate.

Sure enough, as we walked back into the pen, there was Devil, waiting. But this time we were more prepared, and there was no messing around. The moment he pounced I was going to go at him with a head rope. It's easier to noose a croc when they're on the attack because their mouth is open and they're coming straight at you, but you also can't afford to miss. He lunged at me, so I threw the rope, lobbing it over his snout. I pulled it tight and Mick jumped on the rope behind me, pulling hard to keep the tension. But Devil kept coming, moving forward with force.

I shuffled backwards, attempting to push him away from me with the stick in my other hand but he flung his head towards me instead, knocking the stick straight into my chest.

'Arghhhh!' I cried, falling hard onto the concrete and hitting my head. I started seeing stars. By this point, Craig had heard the commotion and had hurried in to help. Mick pulled me to my feet with his free hand, and Craig, Mick and I tugged hard on the rope. We had to be careful with the rough concrete floor beneath us because I didn't want to hurt the croc. I'm always focused on going steady and trying to pull the animal out without banging it up. The last thing I wanted was for the croc to do a death roll and hurt his osteoderms (scales and plates) or crush his brisket. I taped him up with hessian to calm him down and injected the relaxant.

After a period of grace, we lifted Devil and placed him on three connected pallets, before pulling him out and getting the forklift to transport him into the back of the truck with Axel. The 20-tonne excavators were already following in our tracks, bringing down the bricks and concrete pieces. They also knocked down part of the neighbouring pen so we could move in to access the next crocs. We worked our way from pen to pen, wrestling, noosing and relocating the rest of them.

It wasn't like catching a croc in the wild, it was a completely different ball game. Each animal posed its own unique challenge. When you're in their environment, the landscape is less forgiving; there is grass, mud or water, and they are less likely to stress or hurt themselves. Plus, you have space to move or run to if the animal chucks a hissy fit. In a small pen there is limited space and therefore small room for error but we managed to work it out, getting more efficient as we pulled them out one by one. If the forklift was busy helping someone else out, then we would tie the crocs up to nearby trees until we had the equipment to move them to the truck.

I was driving the forklift carrying a big 16-footer, moving it to the truck, when the police turned up. *Oh dear, what have we done? This can't be good*, I thought.

‘G’day, fellas, how you going?’ they asked.

‘Good,’ I said, giving a short answer. From past experience, a copper showing up without an invitation usually resulted in me in the paddy wagon. I didn’t think we were doing anything wrong, we’d got all the right permits sorted but I just know a mountain can be made out of a molehill in these sorts of situations. They walked up right beside the forklift and examined my croc. *Here we go*, I thought.

‘We heard you were in town, mate, wondering if we can get a pic with you and the croc?’ one of them asked.

I felt a rush of relief as my worry subsided and I smiled back at them. *I never thought I’d be so pleased to hear someone ask for a photo with me*, I thought.

‘Oh yeah, of course no worries, lads,’ I said, and hopped out to stand beside them.

We became mates in minutes. ‘Shit, I thought I was in strife and was heading to the lock-up!’ I said.

The coppers laughed. ‘Nah, mate, we just like your show!’ one of them said.

I was relieved. After the first visit, word got around and more locals came down to take pictures of this one-off occasion. So many large crocs lying side-by-side in the one place was a very impressive sight.

Willow joined Mick and me for our last pen of the day, which was a big one. We had to pull five out in one hit and were slowly losing daylight. The first few crocs were easy because they came up out of the water, showing themselves with minimal aggression. They were females and surprisingly easy to handle, especially between the three of us. We poked around in the water and found the large male we were told about, but we couldn't seem to find the last female.

'Maybe there were only four in this pen after all,' I pondered. 'Let's focus on this male then.'

The croc in question was 15 foot but he was a big boy, with the girth you would expect to see on an 18-foot crocodile. He'd showed himself initially but went to ground after further pokes and prods. That's always something you have to be careful of when catching a croc – too many pokes and prods can tire them out, and when they're tired they hide away at the bottom and are near impossible to get out.

I couldn't see him, but I knew he was down towards the middle of the remaining patch of slosh. And then I had an idea.

'This muddy water is dense enough that we should be able to make a bit of a bridge for me to walk across with sheets of tin,' I said.

The guys agreed and went about collecting sticks, pieces of timber and tin sheets. We chucked them out onto the mud and created a pathway so I could get into the middle of the water. The plan was to reach where I imagined the croc to be, poke him with my stick and bring him to the surface. I knew there was the possibility of falling in from the 'bridge', but I preferred to take that chance rather than wading through disease-ridden mud and potentially stepping on the croc in the process.

I walked across the precarious planks and pieces of material, using my stick as support, stepping slow and steady. I was poking and prodding, poking and prodding but nothing was showing up. I submerged my stick next to me and squatted down to realign my balance and that's when I felt myself connect with the croc. It must have been lying right underneath me and it reared up with so much power the makeshift boardwalk went flying into pieces. The croc's tail cleaned me up, lifting me and flinging me to the back of the pen. I swallowed a big gulp of mud in the process, and felt it fill up my ears and trousers. Luckily for me, there was a small concrete ledge that skirted the back of the pen that allowed me to tiptoe back around to the front where Mick and Willow were. I spat out the mud until my guts gave way and, I couldn't take it, I vomited. I looked as if I'd been dipped in chocolate, but it certainly didn't taste like that.

I attempted to wipe the putrid mud from around my eyes and mouth where possible, but with it already all over my hands, I didn't do a very good job. The odour coming off me was terrible, but I wanted to get the croc out sooner rather than later and be done with it.

'There's no time to hose me off and it's not going to do me any good now that I've already swallowed the shit,' I said to Mick and Willow.

The mud was moving around like a mole was burrowing under the soil, so we could see where the croc was. I waded through slowly, like it was quicksand. The movement stopped.

'Ah shit, I hope he's not at my feet,' I said to the boys. 'I'm backing out. Let's build the bridge again, I don't fancy stepping into his jaws.'

So we went again, rebuilding the dodgy platform and I stepped out, this time with a head rope and my stick. I took the first two steps and, in a stroke of luck, he rose to my left. I took the opportunity and gave him a nudge, and he presented his jaws and I noosed him!

'Pull!' I called, as my platform sank and I found myself in knee-deep. The guys pulled him out, meanwhile I prayed his tail didn't swipe and knock me over along the way.

'Matty, move!' Mick yelled. Suddenly, to my left, another croc came at me and had a go at my stick. There WAS one more female!

The boys were battling by themselves, managing to only just keep the croc away from the water. I waded out of the crap and lent a hand, managing to pull the male out relatively easily. We tied him to a nearby tree before the drugs and forklift arrived.

I watched as Craig helped Willow and Mick get the last female out of the hole and we were done for the day. I joined the croc in getting a hose-down. Each time someone got mud on them they cleaned it off, but it was just as important to make sure the crocs were totally hosed down, so they didn't carry any diseases back to the Territory with them. We drove to the local motel and slept off our weariness, ready for day two.

•

There were 10 crocs in two pens left to clear out. We got into it early because we already had the 40 other crocs waiting in the back of the truck. Nick was topping up the sedative drugs every four hours to keep them calm. The truck was parked up in the shade and the crocs were all positioned comfortably with extra layers of hay padding and shade sails pulled over the top, but we still wanted to get the job finished sooner rather than later.

We moved the first out pretty quickly, because we had the entire team helping, which made everything easier. Well, that is, until we came across another cranky male in a pond. All of us were around this pond, all of us had a head rope and all of us had a pole to rouse him up. But every time the croc came up we kept missing! I decided to change tack.

'All right, that's it! I'm going to bring the little excavator in here, park it on the edge, extend the arm and scoop this croc out from a vantage point.'

The guys weren't that keen on this, but I thought it was a good idea, so I ran back and hopped in the excavator and drove it down a small walkway, over an embankment and to the edge of the pond. I edged it down the bank just a bit and soon realised it was a lot steeper than I had anticipated. The excavator began sliding and then started tipping, so I extended the arm with the bucket to stop the machine rolling over. That worked for a second but then the machine was moving sideways and it kept going and going, and I couldn't get the bucket around quick enough. The soil shifted from beneath me and both the machine and I slipped straight into the middle of the pond with the bloody crocodile.

I was sitting in the excavator half submerged in the mud while all of the guys standing around the pond slapped their sticks like crazy, in an attempt to keep the attention away from me. I watched as the croc swirled around in the mud. I was ready to jump on the excavator roof if I needed to.

'Boys, quickly, go grab the chains and the big excavator and help get me out of here!' I yelled.

Craig dropped his stick, ran off and then came straight back, flinging me some chains. I jumped on the roof, hooked up a couple of D-shackles and chucked the chains back to the guys with the big excavator, which had just arrived. I was tempted to try my hand at making it from the excavator to the bank on foot, but I knew how unforgiving the mud was to move through, so I sat myself back in the excavator cab, waiting for the bigger machine to pull me out. Each time the big excavator pulled I looked on at the chains in fear that they would snap, and I'd end up in even deeper shit with the croc. I knew I was slowly sinking, but I still had a small height advantage in the cab. Every so often I saw the croc do a bog lap around me, so I took the opportunity to see if I could coax it up to the surface with a little stick I had with me.

I tried to swipe him with the stick as he went past and the cheeky bastard showed himself all right, launching up and almost ending up in the cab with me! A commotion erupted from the guys as the croc came up for a second crack. His jaw knocked the bottom of the excavator as I finally became airborne, getting lifted to the bank. The croc was so intrigued by the sound of the excavator engine that he followed me up to the bank and the job was made easy. Nick got a head rope on him instantly and Craig, Willow, Seb and Mick pulled the rope off to one side until they got the croc under control.

I didn't say much immediately after that debacle because I wasn't the most liked person that morning, but the guys got over it pretty quickly. We relocated a couple more of them and, in true croc-catching style, finished the operation off with a real pearler.

In the last pen, there was a number of small ponds scattered around the place. We knew there was a male in one of them, but the question was which one. It was hard to pick because this particular enclosure had a heap of two-to three-foot crocs bounding around, so all of the ponds appeared to be pumping with life. (We weren't allowed to catch any of the little ones; they had come from eggs that had accidentally not been collected at the right time, and were going elsewhere.)

Willow, Jono and I did the rounds of the ponds, scoping out where the guy would most likely be hiding. Willow kneeled down at the water's edge of one of the ponds and you wouldn't read about it! The 14-foot croc we were after torpedoed straight towards Willow. He slipped over in the mud and fell flat on his back. But the croc didn't want to attack, it just wanted to get out of the way. Flying at him, it went straight over the top of Willow, using his body as a platform to slide across – over his back, over the top of his shoulders – and pushing off to get a bit more propulsion, slapping him in the face with its tail on the way out.

'Good thing we know where he is,' I said, pointing to the new pond the croc had just entered, but Willow wasn't impressed. We moved along to the pond where there were 10 little crocs darting about the place. They looked like tadpoles in comparison to their big crocodile counterparts that we'd been catching. Still, the two-footers aren't to be taken lightly either, their bite can rip apart muscles in an instant and leave behind a nasty infectious disease, so we had to be careful.

The croc reappeared at the surface of the pond, calmly keeping its distance.

'At least this one isn't playing hide and seek,' Jono said.

I chucked a stone into the pond to see if it would get a reaction and the croc snapped, swiping its tail and cleaning up one of the little crocs along the way. The large croc propelled the fella through the air, and it beelined towards Jono. It hit him square in the chest and knocked him back in the mud, arse over tit. The little croc scurried back into the pond. It was entertaining for us all, but not for Jono, who was in a foul mood and joined Willow for a hose-down. The operation went on for another hour. We secured the last male and one more female, and then we were done.

The local media showed up with the intention of doing a story about the big relocation, but I cut things short because I wanted the crocs moved out ASAP. I pulled out a big fire hose, which was looped up on a spiel attached to a nearby wall, and used it to give the crocs one big spray-down. I added more hay and shading to the inside of the trailer and made sure each croc was safely secured. Then Jono, Mick and I flew to Kununurra, where we waited until the road train arrived and the crocs cleared the border. The customs fella was a bit confused when the cattle truck revealed a mob of crocs, but he signed off on the permits and across the border they went. The boys and I camped the night in Kununurra, leaving at first light, and met the road train at Darwin Crocodile Park at 9 o'clock the next morning.

Unloading the crocs was a hell of a lot easier than catching them, because they were still groggy and emerged from the truck with hardly any resistance. We made ramps so that the crocs could comfortably slide off the backs of the trailers, and once they were off we stretchered them out to their new pens. To this day they are all living happily in Darwin and some of them, one being Axel, have been moved to Crocosaurus Cove, where they live as display and education animals at the popular Darwin tourist attraction. Their new cushy homes are a far cry from their wild west digs.

4

Under investigation

I had five good mates – Matt, Danny, Ben, Changa and AJ – come up to Darwin from down south, all of them eager to get amongst the Territory life and landscape. They were city slickers who had never been up north before and were keen to hook a few barra, chase a couple of hogs and rip about in the chopper. I had planned the ultimate lads' trip.

The southerns stepped out of Darwin Airport with their rosy-cheeked pale faces, bucket hats and fresh Mountain Designs outfits, still with the crease lines from being in the packet. Their shirts certainly hadn't got a workout before, neither had their scuff-free Blundstone boots.

We loaded up the troupe and left Darwin Airport en route to my hangar, where my two choppers were waiting for us to boot out.

'When we get there, I will give you a full safety brief on the choppers and how to operate firearms,' I told them. 'But before we go out for some fun I have to stop off at the shack and check on my genny to make sure she's all good to go for when we get home tonight.'

'No worries, mate. Who's Jenny? Is she your housekeeper?' asked Changa. I was confused, but quickly caught on to what he meant.

'Jesus, old son, genny as in the *generator* that gives the shack power, not a sheila. There's no housekeeper out here, mate, you're going to have to do your own washing and cleaning.'

The troupe erupted with laughter, and the lads started hanging shit on Changa. 'Looks like Changa's buying the first round at the pub tonight!'

After dropping our gear at the shack and checking out the genny I introduced the boys to Tripod, my 17-foot pet crocodile, which they couldn't quite comprehend either.

'Wow, Matty, that's one hell of a statue, it looks so real.'

'Ohhhh, ya shitting me, aren't ya?!'

They think he's made of concrete, I thought to myself.

I decided to play along. 'All right, lads, let's get a picture.'

I got the guys close enough to Tripod and asked Crab, my other chopper pilot, to get a picture of us. Just as everyone was smiling for the camera I flicked a rock next to Tripod's head and he exploded with an almighty snap, slamming his jaws down and splashing water over everyone. I've never seen a bunch of blokes scream like that before, running in the opposite direction.

'Righty-o, you lot, into the choppers,' I said, once they'd

calmed down. 'It's time to give Tripod a feed and get some bait for my croc traps.'

The guys piled into the choppers and we flew over a 25,000-hectare cattle station, located south of Dundee in the Northern Territory, and a prime location for catching feral pigs. We saw mobs of pigs running beneath us, like ants scurrying around on a hot day.

'There's over 20 million of these guys spread across Australia, and they're a big problem around here,' I explained to Matt, Danny and Ben, who were in my chopper. 'They're feral pests and they muck up the land, spreading weeds and destroying the habitat of our native animals, so I don't mind using a few for croc bait.'

The NT and other state governments spend millions of dollars every year trying to manage the feral pig population through baited trapping, mustering and aerial culling. So when it comes time to set my croc traps, feral pigs are the most accessible and sustainable bait there is.

Crab was flying Changa and AJ in the second chopper, following me closely behind. We stopped a couple of times so the boys could get their eyes in with a few pot shots at termite mounds. After everyone had become more acquainted with their guns, we got back into the air and found a good mob of pigs in a swamp adjacent to the river.

'Oi, Crab, I'm going to land here and I want you to drop your lads off next to me, fly back up and scoot around those pigs. There's a couple of good boars I want to get,' I said over the radio as I landed my chopper. 'Give me a moment to shut down and get the boys in position. Just make sure you keep those pigs bailed up in the cane grass and try not to bring too many at us at once. I don't want to get hit up the nuts here.'

'Roger,' Crab radioed back.

Pigs are pretty easy to muster. Like with cattle, you drop in behind with the chopper, pushing them to clear open ground. You stay low in the trees and drive them out using the down-wash of the chopper. They move slowly through the swamps but as soon as they're out into the open, they bolt.

I got the guys lined up in a formation where they wouldn't be at risk of shooting themselves or the chopper. In the past, I've had guests accidentally shoot my helicopter, blow its skids off or almost shoot themselves in the foot. And sometimes the gun jams, there's a misfire, or in the heat of the moment they just get completely overwhelmed and the hog gets the upper hand. These past experiences make me very savvy when it comes to safety precautions.

I called Crab on my handheld radio: 'You're up, mate!'

Crab began mustering the first group of hogs out of the waterhole and towards us. The plan was for the guys to hit them before the hogs got across the plain to the river. I made sure the group of five blokes was shooting in a northerly direction, away from the river or anywhere there could be fishermen. My palms were getting clammy just watching the guys, so I could only imagine the sweat building on their hands as they saw the chopper in the background and the cane grass moving about with the pigs within. It could be an angry boar, a group of piglets or even a raging buffalo. Everyone was fidgeting in their stance.

'Take your time, focus, and be calm and steady with your shot,' I said with a raised, stern voice. 'One good shot outweighs 10 bad ones.'

The first group of pigs emerged from the cane grass, coming at us, grunting in the distance. There were mostly sows and smaller pigs, which was a good start, but I could see a big boar at the back.

'Hold your fire, hold your fire. Wait, wait!' I yelled out to the guys.

Once the pigs got within 20 metres of the boys, I called, 'Fire!'

And away they shot. Cracks went out and the smell of gunpowder filled the air. I saw two pigs fall, while the big boar continued to trail at the back. A couple more cracks of the rifles and the boar fell too.

'No time to rest, guys, reload and get ready. The next mob is coming,' I advised. Before I could finish my sentence Crab had another four big boars beelining straight towards us.

'Bend those pigs, Crab!' I shouted on the radio.

It was too late. The boars had lined us up and I screamed again, 'Fire, fire, fire!' Another two went down, but the other two were charging. I grabbed Changa's rifle and quickly jammed a round, letting the closest one have it. He fell, and I quickly reloaded and took a shot from my hip, dropping the second pig just as it reached my feet.

'Wow. Well, that was exciting, wasn't it, boys?'

Crab landed and we sorted the six pigs. The boys were having a big barney about who shot the biggest one. It was comical. We hooked the pigs up to the chopper and Crab slung them back to the traps. It was happy days. Or so I thought . . .

•

It just so happened that a local fishing guide – let's call him Scott – had seen my choppers flying around that day. Scott was running charters in the area and from all accounts wasn't too happy with the competition from my new adventure tourism business I had opened not far from where he operated. Apparently Scott was on the floodplains of the river the same morning we were out shooting and heard the guns going off. Coincidentally he also saw choppers that he presumed were mine, even though he had never met me or seen my choppers before. He just saw a chopper and thought, *That's Matt Wright*, and made up a story to go with it.

I got a call the next day and I was ropable.

'Matt, it's Darren here from the NT police department. We've got a report from a bloke called Scott who said you were flying around recklessly in a chopper and shooting at his fishing charter boats with an automatic rifle.'

'Ya kidding me, right?' I snapped back at the cops.

'Well, were you out flying in that area?' Darren asked.

'Yeah, I was, actually, but I wasn't shooting at no fishing charter. If I was, I wouldn't miss. What a tosser!'

I couldn't believe it. I didn't see anyone else out there and the supposed 'fully automatic rifle' he was talking about was probably the sound of our five rifles shooting simultaneously at the pigs. I made certain that we were on private property and away from people. It was just another case of tall poppy syndrome that seems to be rife in Australia.

I understand the cops were doing their due diligence but, unfortunately for me, this petty complaint led to a long and serious investigation that started from that afternoon and continued on for the next few years. But I didn't let the lads know what had happened and made sure they enjoyed the rest of their trip to the NT.

•

The saying 'when it rains it pours', I swear, was written with me in mind. Not only was I under investigation for a shooting incident that didn't happen, but I also had lawyers going in all sorts of directions with a CASA court case into my flying on *Outback Wrangler* and an ex-girlfriend trying to take me to court for a stack of money after a 12-month relationship. The investigation into the pig-shooting incident had dragged on for just over three years. I'd been in and out of the cop shop, answering silly questions and giving evidence. Finally, on Tuesday, 11 November 2014, I was going to pick up two coppers from Sandpalms resort in Bynoe Harbour, fly them to the area where the reports were made and show them the guns we were shooting with. The cops needed to do this one last time before the case was closed and I was really looking forward to laying it all to rest. But the day was far from restful – there were coppers, choppers, chainsaws and a monster croc. It was an absolute clusterfuck.

This final visit from the cops was in the middle of filming for season two of *Outback Wrangler*. Jono, Willow, me and my other good mate Craig were all camping out at a large cattle station, along with the camera crew. The lads and I had already pulled out and relocated four crocs from the area, but there was one massive croc left to go. And it was this croc that was causing the most damage to cattle. I thought it would be a quick enough job and that I'd be out of there by lunchtime, ready to meet the coppers at Sandpalms.

'All right, fellas, hop on this off-roader Polaris and head down to the landing, sort out the airboat and grab the gear we need for the swamp. I'll get the chopper ready just in case we need it,' I said to the guys.

I flew the chopper and landed it near the water so I was ready to boot out of there when the time came. We didn't know what to expect because we'd never done a relocation using an airboat. It would have been an easy job if we'd been able to access the waterhole by foot, pull the croc out and put it straight onto a trailer. But this particular croc was in an area completely encased by jungle, so we had to cut our way through dense foliage to get the airboat in there.

We had two chainsaws, duct tape, rope, a harpoon and stick at the ready. I was driving, and Willow and Jono were on the chainsaws. Craig and our cameraman, Ash, as well as our second cameraman, producer and sound guy followed us on foot along the bank as we tracked the airboat through the thick paperbark swamps at a snail's pace. Every so often we'd make a little break, but we'd soon be stopped again by the paperbarks and floating logs. It was quite obvious that no person had ever been here before.

I made a sharp turn on the airboat and it got stuck on some floating mat, which is a dense, free-floating weed. The airboat hitched up on an angle, tipping Jono and me overboard, along with the two chainsaws.

'Shit! Move quickly and scoop up those chainsaws,' Willow yelled from the boat.

I was wide-eyed and couldn't believe what had just happened.

Jono on the other hand thought it was all a bit of fun. 'At least we've got the chainsaws to fend off the crocs,' he joked.

I forced a laugh. We managed to grab the chainsaws and waded towards the airboat. The rest of the lads were on the bank at this point, telling us to get a move on, knowing full well what lay beneath the water. The floating mat made it difficult to move quickly. It felt like I was trying to walk against a strong current of water, and I was second-guessing whether I was actually making any progress. After a very long five minutes of unease we finally made it onto the boat unscathed.

It was the beginning of the wet season in the Territory so it was 39 degrees Celsius with 90 per cent humidity. It was 11 a.m., not even the peak of the heat, and everyone was already giving me daggers. By this point we had spent three hours cutting down trees and got as far as 300 metres, with at least a kilometre to go. We made progress with another 10-metre stretch until the blade broke on Jono's chainsaw. At the same time, I heard Willow cursing next to me – he'd got his chainsaw completely stuck in the trunk of a 10-inch paperbark and it wasn't coming out. What a fucking disaster. Willow was sweating bullets, Jono's humour had dried up, I was quiet and it was the first time I'd ever seen Craig crack it. We were all exhausted and grumpy.

'Is this worth it? What happens if we get there and the croc's not even in the waterhole?' Willow whined.

He had a point, but I'd promised Paul, the station's owner, that I'd get the croc out for him and now was the only opportunity we had. My gut told me the croc was there and that we'd find him, and besides, a bit of hard work never hurt anyone. I knew I had that meeting soon and I'd have to get on the bank and bolt back to my chopper on foot to get there in time. Jono persisted with the stuck chainsaw, using a small pocketknife to hack it out of the tree. We sat there exhausted and watched and waited until finally the chainsaw came free – it was 12.30 p.m. by this point.

'All right, lads, you keep trucking. I've got to head over to Sandpalms. I'll be gone for about an hour but hopefully by the time I'm back you'll be in the waterhole and I'll come and find you.' No one said a word as I jumped onto the bank and returned to the chopper. They were pissed off and I don't blame them.

I flew over to Sandpalms. I knew I needed to return bearing gifts so I could earn some brownie points with the guys back at the swamp, so I borrowed an esky from Sandpalms and packed the bottom of it with cold beers, followed by a layer of ice, then Powerade, bottled water and some more ice. Then I picked up the coppers. They were great people and were keen to get everything closed off, so after a quick fly around and debrief they were ready to head home.

'Guys, you don't mind if I just fly over a swamp here on the way back and check in on my boys?' I asked the two cops. 'They're on an airboat trying to catch a croc.'

'Of course not, mate. Would be interesting to have a look, anyway,' the sheila cop said.

We flew in low to the waterhole and I couldn't believe it! The guys had made it through the jungle, and there was Jono, on the edge of the airboat with a stick, poking the water as it erupted with a huge crocodile. Behind Jono was the rest of the crew, violently waving me down.

'I'm sorry, guys,' I said to the police, 'but I'm going to have to land here and make my way to the waterhole to catch this croc. You're welcome to follow.'

I landed the chopper and started running through the trees along the bank with the esky in hand and the cops close on my tail. They sounded like a marching band, with their tasers, batons and guns banging and clanging as they ran.

'Make sure you don't get your gear hung up on the vines and taser yourself,' I yelled. I finally saw the lads through the clearing, and they were beaming from ear to ear. Boy, they looked absolutely cooked, but their energy levels had sure as hell lifted. Jono had got the croc on the end of the harpoon, and was waiting for my call. The croc was situated between heaps of floating mat and fallen melaleuca trees with six feet of water beneath. It had nowhere to go, but it was going to be one hell of a battle to get him out and onto the airboat.

'Take a break, lads, the croc's not going anywhere. He'll just lie here, he's got nowhere to go.'

The lads sighed with relief as I chucked them all a Powerade and a bottle of water. I was back in the good books. The condensation on the bottles and the sweat dripping off of their heads would have made for a great TV ad.

But then soon it was back to work. Craig made his way over near the floating mat, taking hold of one side of the croc, while Jono and I perched up on a fallen tree that was sticking out across the water. We had to leverage the croc's head up to get a rope around its snout, but it was proving to be difficult.

And then, without warning, the croc flung up and grabbed the tree branch sticking out between Jono and me. It wobbled and we lost our footing, falling onto the floating mat and sinking into the water. We hoisted ourselves back onto the tree quick-smart with the croc in sight. With all this action going on, it was our cameraman Ash who had the hardest job of us all – bouncing around between the airboat, the landing, the floating mat and the tree, trying to get the best shot, at the same time as making sure he didn't lose his camera or an arm. Every now and then I spotted the coppers in my periphery. I don't think either of them knew what to do, so they just stood there frozen in shock, with wide eyes and gaping mouths.

Finally, we managed to get the head rope on the croc when it came up for a breath of air. We got its head up the side of the airboat and, luckily for us, the croc's mouth was already bound up with weeds from death-rolling underwater, which made taping its mouth shut heaps easier. Craig and I jumped into the waterhole with the croc while Jono and Willow pulled the rope, but we had to get some behind-the-scenes help from the *Outback Wrangler* crew. The lads put down their tools and gave us a hand to lift the croc up onto the deck of the airboat. The job was done and it was time to head home with the croc on the airboat, but not before the coppers got a selfie with this monster croc.

5

Operation Congo

On the edge of the Democratic Republic of the Congo and Tanzania border is Lake Tanganyika, an immense body of water with outflowing rivers full of wildlife. In 2010, South African Johannes Hendrik Coetzee or 'Hendri', a hero in the world of whitewater exploration, set out on what would be his last ever paddling expedition. His in-depth knowledge of the area resulted in people saying he was the man who possessed the 'key to the Congo'. Hendri guided two American expedition paddlers, Ben Stookesberry and Chris Korbulic, on an epic kayaking adventure through central Africa. It is because of my friendship with Chris that I know the story I am about to tell you.

The trio started in Uganda and paddled through a series of rapids along the Ruzizi River and then water-taxied across Lake Tanganyika to the outflowing Lukuga River. The region has seen decades of bloody battles where millions of lives were taken and thousands of deceased bodies were disposed of in the waterways. This dark history means the large crocs in the river acquired a taste for human flesh and, given the abundance of food, they grew to incredible sizes. One croc, whom the locals call Gustave, is reported to be an incredible 20 feet long and has eaten in excess of 300 people. And Gustave isn't alone; he has lots of scaly mates who are 16- to 18-foot alpha predators with a liking for humans.

Hendri, Chris and Ben journeyed down the Lukuga River, stopping off at villages along the way. At each stop, travellers and locals warned them of a man-eating crocodile hanging out in the waters where they were headed. This sort of story wasn't anything special for someone like Hendri – he knew about the risks involved with the crocodiles in the Congo but accepted that it was just part of the adventure.

They were travelling in November, the end of the dry season, when the water was at its lowest and the heat was at its highest. Hippos wallowed around, posing their own danger, and the crocs were starting to become even more territorial as their nesting season approached.

The boys came up to a section in the river that Hendri called the 'supermarket'. It was an expression he used to describe where the dead water pooled at the end of a fast-flowing rapid. This was where crocs would hang out, waiting for something to get caught up to feast on. When they reached the 'supermarket', Hendri told Chris and Ben to keep paddling until the crocs were gone and the river had widened out. Ben was in the lead, followed closely by Hendri, with Chris lagging behind a little. Two crocs launched from the banks thrashing into the water and Hendri called out to Chris: 'Come on, mate, catch up and get in front of me, keep moving and keep the pace up.' Chris got up alongside the left of Hendri and, as he overtook him, he remembers hearing Hendri say in a weird, matter-of-fact way, 'Oh my god.' As Chris turned his head to see what was going on, he saw an image that would stay with him for the rest of his life.

A croc's head, the same size as Hendri's torso, emerged from the water and grabbed Hendri, slowly pulling him upside down into the murky water. It dragged him underwater so laxly that there was barely a splash.

Chris was in so much shock that he completely froze for a moment, but then snapped out of it, turned his kayak and powered over to Hendri's kayak, which was spinning around in circles. Feeling utterly helpless and shocked about what had just happened, Chris took a few jabs under water, trying to hit the animal. Ben frantically made his way over to Chris to give him a hand, but the chaos stopped and the kayak appeared empty.

Hendri was gone.

Ben and Chris paddled for their lives and got out of the water as soon as they saw a small clearing on the riverbank. They were dwarfed by the tall cane grass and could see nothing but jungle in front of them. I can only imagine how helpless they would have felt at that moment. Their safety net had just been torn open, they were alone in the middle of nowhere and the one person who knew how to conquer the Congo was gone. They had no choice but to get back in their kayaks and continue to race downstream. They got very lucky – only a few more clicks along the river, they came to a bridge. It was the only bridge they had seen in days, and situated alongside it, was a small grass hut village called Kabeya Maji.

Chris and Ben paddled their kayaks up to a makeshift washing bay and ran up the banks yelling out to the locals, 'Crocodile! Crocodile!' They communicated in basic French with the help of hand gestures, explaining what had happened, with Chris raising his arms and clapping them down repeatedly to mimic the jaws of a croc. A few of the men from the village started taking their shirts off to go for a swim and investigate.

'No, no, no, just wait, just wait,' Ben urged them to stay. He begged the village chief for a motorised boat to take them back upstream to look for Hendri, but they quickly learnt that the village had no boats. The locals had stopped using water travel after several of them had been pulled overboard and eaten by a big croc in the area. They told Ben and Chris that eight people had been taken in six years. The guys realised in that moment that they had no hope of finding their mate's body.

The guys sat on the bank helplessly as Chris told Ben what he had witnessed.

'I saw the whole thing happen. The croc came out of the water, it was massive.'

'It got him by the shoulder?'

'Yeah, just there.' Chris signalled to his left shoulder.

They watched as Hendri's kayak drifted downstream towards them. The village people recovered the boat, but sadly Hendri's remains were never found.

It wasn't easy for Chris and Ben to return home to America; they had to stay in the Congo and wait around for a hearing, conducted by the United Nations, into Hendri's death. The guys spoke, in front of the tribunal, reliving the trauma and describing the incident, blow by blow. They had to stay in the country for another week until the case was finally cleared and they were allowed to leave. Chris and Ben flew out and spent a week in Jinja, Uganda, with Hendri's friends before going home.

•

In August 2011, while I was doing some flying work in the Yukon region in Canada, I got a call from a guy at the National Geographic Channel who explained what had happened to Hendri.

'Matt, we're wondering if you'd be interested in heading to the Congo in three months to do a show on catching and relocating this man-eating crocodile?' He spoke with a hybrid accent; not quite American, not quite English, so I figured he must be from the global headquarters. I wasn't really thinking about the trip or the show, I was in shock at what I'd just heard about Hendri.

'Sure, I would be really interested in the project, but what do Hendri's mates and family think?' I was keen to do the job but I wanted to speak with Chris and Ben and get their perspectives before committing.

The next day I found myself on Skype talking to Chris and Ben, and listening to a raw rendition of events. Ben led the conversation, and there was no sensationalism or drama in what he said, only real emotion. I felt his sadness and connected with his calmness and sincerity.

'Hendri spent a lot of time in the Congo and it was a dream of his to build a well in Kabeya Maji so people can access fresh water without having to go to the riverbank and risk being eaten. We want to go back and build the well as well as catch and relocate the crocodile, but we need your help with the croc part.'

I was sold on the trip and confirmed my involvement with Nat Geo that day.

I couldn't shake the thought of Hendri being engulfed in the jaws of a croc and how painful and overwhelming his last moments would have been. Chris sent through photos, videos and diaries from the trip, including footage of Hendri being taken that Ben had captured on a GoPro strapped to his head. I also viewed the intense footage from the United Nations hearing – the guys had really been through the thick of it. I spent hours on the phone to our African film crew and a personal guide, also known as a fixer, on the ground in the Congo, explaining the ins and outs of catching a croc. I emailed the fixer pictures and descriptions of the traps and harpoons I needed so we could hit the ground running. I started tracking the weather and researching the region.

I worked out that November was the perfect time to travel because it would be hot with low water, which meant crocodiles would be out on the banks, not deep in the water. Chris and Ben agreed, and were familiar with the conditions at that time of year because it had almost been 12 months since they were in the Congo when Hendri was taken.

Come November, everything was in place – visas were sorted, flights were booked and I had my yellow fever shot. I was ready to fly out when I received an unexpected call from Nat Geo informing me the trip had been cancelled. I was aware of the political unrest building in the Congo but I thought that was part and parcel of visiting that part of the world, so I didn't think it would affect our trip. It was the lead-up to the December 2011 presidential and parliamentary elections, and the riots were building every day. People were getting killed in political rallies and that was only the beginning. Nat Geo knew that if the local people didn't accept who won it was going to get worse, and it did.

I was disappointed we couldn't go, but seeing what unfolded in the Congo, I was glad to be home in Australia for the time being. I flew back to Darwin and started work collecting crocodile eggs, and kept in contact with the producer from Nat Geo. She was adamant that the trip would still go ahead, but we just had to wait until the country was more stable and the weather more favourable. Our fixer on the ground in the Congo advised that February would be an appropriate time to visit, with kind weather and a calmer political situation.

I was sceptical from the get-go because the seasons in the Congo line up with what we have in Darwin, and February is the peak of the wet season; meaning high water and thunderstorms, which is the shittiest conditions for spotting a croc, let alone catching one. But Nat Geo trusted their fixer because they'd used him before. He knew the country and the people in power, so he could handle the logistics and politics without too many headaches. When I questioned the fixer about the time of year and the weather, he insisted it would be hot and dry with low water and crocodiles everywhere, so we went with his intel and booked our second attempt. I brought Mick Burns along with me – he's an experienced croc wrangler and I needed another set of hands.

Mick and I, along with our crew, landed in Johannesburg, South Africa, to discover that the fixer hadn't fixed anything. It turned out the visas hadn't been sorted and there was no one to meet us. The rest of the crew were in the same boat so our producer, assistant producer, cameraman, second cameraman, soundy, Chris, Ben, me and Mick were all stuck in the customs office. After a few phone calls, we managed to get cleared but missed our connecting flight. There wasn't another flight for quite some time, so we had to hang around in Johannesburg for a week.

The airport motel was less than ideal, with ceilings covered in mould that resembled moss, grumpy staff and corridors that echoed voices, footsteps and doors. We were well and truly ready to get out by the seventh day. Nat Geo arranged a charter flight for our crew to fly direct to the town of Kalemie, located next to the mouth of Lakuga River. We were eager to board the plane and arrived safely at the other end, where we finally met up with our fixer in person.

I'm impatient at the best of times and value time more than anything – I absolutely hate wasting it. And after all the delays we'd experienced, I was recharged and ready to hook in.

'So, mate, lets grab the gear and equipment and hit the ground running, hey?'

Our fixer stared blankly back at me. 'I haven't had the chance to get your equipment sorted yet, so we'll do that over the next few days.' He wasn't asking me, he was telling me.

I wanted to react, but I didn't want to rock the already rocky boat. 'I guess that's our only option then.'

I couldn't believe it. We were meant to have harpoons, ropes and steel for traps, and we didn't have a fucking thing. He could sense how pissed off I was, so he disappeared and came back half an hour later with what he said was steel. I raised my knee and pulled down on the steel panel. It looked like steel and kind of felt like steel, but it sure wasn't steel. It bent like a plastic fork and snapped. I didn't have to say anything, I just turned to the fixer.

He seemed nervous. 'There's heaps of other stuff, mate, don't worry. Leave it with me.'

But I wasn't about to let him waste any more time. 'I don't know about that idea, how about WE have a look around.'

We set off together and found some sturdy old gates, bamboo and chicken wire in a shonky little hardware store. I still needed a harpoon pole, so the fixer organised for two of the locals to cut down a tree and make four poles. When I saw how eager they were to do the work and make some extra money, I couldn't say no. I shot myself in the foot a bit because it took them another two days to whittle down the wood for the harpoons, which meant more waiting, but it was worth it. All they'd used was a small knife and sandpaper, but I'd never seen anything like it. The poles were completely smooth and as straight as a die. Our boat and trailer arrived soon after, and then we packed up our three banged-up four-wheel drives, ready for our nine-hour journey through open savannah country to Kabeya Maji.

It was a wet and bumpy ride along winding roads – or what passed for roads – in the Congo. They were muddy and hard to make out. I felt like I was back home in Darwin during a wet season monsoon; we were engulfed by grey and the rain was pelting down. The rain subsided for a couple of hours, so I got on the back of the truck and took in the landscape – the striking blue skies and towering cumulus clouds were pretty special. I could taste the heavy damp air and felt the humidity sticking to my skin. We took the opportunity to do some introductory pieces to camera for the show.

'The boys have been in a very tough situation. There was nothing they could have done to save Hendri – you've got absolutely no chance when you're up against something of that size deep in the water,' I explained. 'It will be good for the guys to go back to where everything happened and see with a clear head how impossible it would have been to do anything for Hendri once he was taken.'

I got in the four-wheel drive with everyone and we drove off. We stopped a couple of times for a hot beer and a quick stretch, then kept on trucking. The rain started to pour down again just as we reached the Lakuga River crossing. Our fixer told us that we would need to put our cars onto a ferry, which would take us to the other side of the river.

The 'ferry' wasn't what any of us expected. As I watched it approach I couldn't believe my eyes. It was comprised of four large canoes strapped together with a steel sheet laid across the top, creating a platform. There was a man on the front and back of each canoe using large bamboo pole to leverage the ferry across the river.

By this point, the rain was building and I couldn't see further than two feet in front of me. 'I don't know about this, I can't see how this dinky thing is going to transport a car full of gear and all of us.'

I love adventure but this just seemed silly to me – the current in the river looked strong, and I had a good idea of how many crocs would be waiting, ready for a feed if we fell in.

'There's no other option to get us over to the other side, I've done this lots of times before and haven't ever had a problem.' The fixer seemed confident, but I was frustrated that I had to put our fate into his hands when I already didn't trust him.

The car drove over a steel ramp that connected the river-bank to the do-it-yourself ferry and we got on. There were holes and leaks in all of the canoes.

I tried to make light of the situation: 'Okay, I'll plug my finger into this hole and we'll be right to go, hey?!'

A couple of nervous laughs came from the camera crew.

'All right, Chris, are you ready?' I called out to Chris, who was at the front of the boat. He had been given a bucket to bail out water from the most damaged canoe so that we wouldn't sink as we moved across the river.

'Yup, let's do this!' he shouted back.

The moody current jerked the ferry in different directions but we finally made it downstream and hit into the bank on the other side of the river. Everyone looked relieved.

We travelled for another hour and made it across the bridge and into the village of Kabeya Maji. Silhouettes of wispy clouds spread across the big sun, which had sunk halfway behind the horizon. Ben and Chris were both pretty emotional as we crossed the bridge near where their friend had been taken.

'It's nice to arrive at Hendri's favourite part of the day, sunset. He always stopped to appreciate the magic in it,' Ben said.

Chris nodded. 'After spending seven weeks with him I knew he was someone inspiring, who I would call a very good friend.'

•

The unknown is the greatest thing about adventure but unfortunately in the case of what happened to Hendri, Ben and Chris had no way of knowing that their expedition was going to go horribly wrong. Waking up on my first morning in Kabeya Maji, I was filled with that same excitement of not knowing what would be in store for me during my next month in the Congo. I was aware of the potential danger, but confident in my own abilities.

I woke up at 4.30 with butterflies in my belly. But before we went anywhere, I had to slaughter a goat for bait. I'd bought a goat from the local people for a lot of money (it worked out to be about 100 Australian dollars, which is out of control!), went to a quiet area and put the goat down with a sharp knife. I came back to camp with fresh meat for dinner and bait for the traps. We got going at dawn, and our first stop was the river's 'supermarket' stretch, where Hendri had disappeared.

Ben and Chris came out with Mick and me to show us exactly where it had happened. The camera crew followed along as the boys retold the story to camera.

'When you put kayaks in the water in the Congo, you know you're paddling into sketchy territory and, equally so, the locals who fetch water along the riverbanks know they're entering the kill zone,' Ben told me. He was right – locals will continue to go about their day-to-day business and will continue to get chewed unless the croc is removed. The river is such an integral part of their lives and culture that they'd rather run the risk of being eaten than give up their lifestyle.

We reached the 'supermarket', where there was an island created by the swollen river.

'That's where we'll look at setting a big trap.' I pointed to a cleared-out space on the island bank. 'I'm sure we could lure him there with bait.'

Our driver banked our boat and the cameraman and soundy followed us onto the island. The guys were being too complacent, turning their backs to the water. It was putting me on edge. I was used to being on crocodile nests or in the swamps with guys who knew about crocodiles, but this time it was just Mick and me and four guys who were completely green.

'Just stay away from the edge of the water!' I warned. 'If it's not a croc it will be a hippo, and you'll be breakfast.' I turned to Mick. 'Pass me the bait and we'll wedge it up here.' I pointed to a tree situated about five or so metres from the water.

Mick lugged the fresh goat meat out of the boat and I clambered up the tree. He passed me the bait and I hung it in the branches so that the blood and guts dripped all over the ground. Then it was time to set the motion-sensor cameras. I strapped them in, tested them and tilted them up and down until I was satisfied with their position.

It's difficult to measure the exact size of an animal on camera. Certain angles can be deceiving, making animals look three times their actual size. Mick paced out two metres directly in front of the water, then paced out another five metres towards the baited tree from the bank. I knocked some pegs in the ground as Mick walked. The markers would help us better identify the size of the croc on camera when it approached the bait. Then we got back in the boat and travelled downstream, even closer towards where Hendri was taken, to set the second bait. It was an eerie feeling looking around and seeing no signs of wildlife – not a monkey, not a mozzie, barely a bird in the sky. It didn't seem right, we were in the heart of the Congo and the environment was dead. We pulled up and set more motion-sensor cameras in the area then headed home.

On the way, we approached the bridge hanging over the river, with green banks on either side and open sky stretching out behind. A group of locals greeted us at the wash bay, an inlet of shallow water on the riverbanks where they washed their clothes. It was a peaceful scene until the water moved. I jumped out of the boat and into the muddy water, grabbing hold of a lively three-foot salty. The locals looked at me like I was mad as I pulled it out of the water.

'If this little guy is hanging around here, then his mum and dad won't be far away, either,' I explained.

Chris and Ben relayed my words in their basic French to the village chief and the locals around them, but they didn't seem too worried. Crocs were part of daily life. They weren't concerned about the smaller crocs, they just wanted us to catch the big guy. I strapped another couple of cameras on the bamboo around the wash bay with the hope of building a picture of croc activity on the village doorstep.

'We know what makes crocs tick – the first step is finding

proof the big croc is still around and then we'll go from there,' Mick said to camera.

•

We finished setting up our gear and operations in the chief's compound then went to meet some of the locals who had experienced close calls with crocs. So far the local victims had all been fishermen, and there was one lucky escapee who had come face to face with a big croc a few months earlier while he was out fishing with his brother. Chris, Ben and I went to meet the victim and his brother in their mud grass hut.

'My brother fell and the crocodile bit his leg. It swallowed his leg up to here.' The brother pointed to his knee.

'Was the croc trying to pull you in to the water?' Chris asked the victim in French. Ben translated his response for me.

'Yes, the crocodile bit down on my leg and tried to pull me in. I held on to a rock and my brother grabbed a big stick and put it in the crocodile's mouth.'

'He was only this far from the water then the croc let go.' The brother gestured an inch in the air with his fingers pinched closely together.

We also wanted to know more about the croc because they would have got a good view of him out of the water.

'How big was it?' Chris asked.

'As big as the room!' The guy became very animated and threw his arms in the air. The room was about 16 feet wide.

'The size matches the croc that took Hendri,' Ben concluded.

We wrapped up work for the day and set up our tents in a cluster in the middle of the village. After just one night of camping out and eating around the fire I really got a sense of their lives. It is based solely around the basics: shelter, fire, food and water.

•

The next morning I had to take Ben and Chris out again with the camera crew in our shadow.

'If any of you end up in the water, get down as low as you can to the river floor and swim silently without making a noise or splash until you get to the bank,' I warned the guys.

Our boat had a motor but it was essentially a rubber dinghy, which a croc could puncture in a heartbeat, and our local driver was apprehensive.

'Chris and Ben, when we get up there, just make sure you hold the bamboo poles in your hands for protection,' I instructed.

We got on the island and before we could prepare the cameras we could see evidence in the mud: claw marks, a smaller print and a bigger print.

'It looks like about a seven-foot and a 12-foot croc,' Mick said. 'There are some smooth lines here, so I imagine the 12-footer has wiped out the little one.'

'Oi! Stay a couple of metres back from that water . . . more! Step back more, stand there!' I called to Chris and Ben. They were both extremely capable fellas, but you can't learn about crocs overnight so I was constantly on the lookout for them.

We switched out the sensor cameras as the rain started pelting down around us.

'We'll check this footage on the laptop. But the crocs are obviously hungry,' said Mick. 'He would definitely be in this area, it's just a matter of time,' he added.

'This section of the river always creeps me out,' Chris said.

'Yeah, it has a spooky feel to it, and this rain is adding some intensity. The good thing is that rains like this bring crocs to the surface because they enjoy the showering sensation, so hopefully we'll get the big fella,' I reasoned.

'All right, lads, come on, let's get out of here. We don't want to be hanging around here too long with this heavy rain,' Mick said.

We tracked back to the village in the boat. It was quiet and I could feel everyone thinking. We got off at the wash bay and I walked up to the bridge and looked down at the river.

It was peaceful. An old man paddled quietly along the bank, hunting for some food. I could hear the faint noise of his canoe's slipstream and watched the pretty little whirlpools coming off the backs of his handcrafted paddles. Every couple of minutes a small patch of bubbles rose to the surface in scattered spots across the river. The man looked around. He knew the crocs were there but he didn't seem worried. He looked up at me and smiled, and I smiled back. In the distance I could hear the village kids playing and laughing and I watched as the farmers on the other side of the river dug into the ground with their homemade garden tools – a rock attached to a hard stick, crafted into an axe-like shape for digging. The village was a harmonious community – the only problem was its unwelcome members lurking in the water.

The old man enjoyed the river, pulling up fish and paddling along when he was out of luck. He secured another catch and fist-pumped into the air. He was so proud of himself. He hauled it up, and as the fish exited the water so did a dark black shadow. Out launched a crocodile, taking the man's fish and snapping his line. The man didn't jump back or react, he just sat down and accepted the steal. He peered over the boat for a moment then put his thumbs up to me to show he was okay.

We got in and downloaded all of the footage onto my laptop. The first lot of action was two crocs, just like Mick had guessed, coming over to investigate the bait. The next slide was a big hippo approaching the island. It hopped up onto the bank, wandered around and sniffed the bait then turned sideways to the water, tilted its head back and opened its jaws right up.

'That looks like a territorial move,' said Chris. 'It wouldn't surprise me if it was facing off with the croc in the water, staring it down.'

Chris was right. The hippo moved out, and a couple of slides later one hell of a croc crept out from the water.

'Wow, that's the sort of croc we're looking for.' Mick was impressed. We sized it up to our markers on the ground and left it up to Mick to determine its measurements. 'There's no question that animal is a metre wide. That's really big, I reckon about 15 to 16 feet long. That's a good-sized crocodile.'

I clicked to the next slide.

'Oh shit, that's crazy!' Ben couldn't believe it. The very next shot, less than 10 minutes after the croc disappeared, was us pulling up in our boat.

'That's the scary thing, if we go back to that area there could be a croc loitering. Or if that hippo's hiding in the bushes, he'll come at us and those things can run 30 miles an hour, they're even worse than crocs,' Chris said. 'Out of all the footage from the three locations, the island has the most activity so let's focus on that.'

The rest of the team agreed and we hit the sack early, ready for the morning.

•

I spoke to camera the next day on the way back to the island, as it was important for me to explain to the general public why I wanted to catch this croc.

'My work is about more than just helping the village; it's about saving animals, relocating and protecting them. Not destroying them or their environment. If these attacks keep continuing, the croc will be shot, which is not what I want. If we can take him out and move him to a nearby park in South Africa, where the owners have said they would love to have him, then to me that's a job well done.'

Mick and I hooked in getting the trap sorted, and the boys came and lent a hand a couple of hours later. I created a box with fence panels and bamboo. It was a simple enclosure that mimicked the same design as the traps I made in Australia – three walls and a gate tied together. I put bait on the end of a piece of rope, which would then trigger the gate to drop down when the rope was pulled. I baited the rope with more goat meat and dug a narrow channel so that the crocs could get in and the hippos stayed out.

I overheard Chris speaking to camera, sceptical about the trap: 'I mean, it seems like it'll work. We'll wait and see, I guess.'

I yelled back to him, 'Oh, it'll work, mate!'

But then big rains came in and so we had to steam back to camp faster than usual.

We were heading along the river when I heard Mick call out, 'Stop!' I turned and saw our cameraman falling overboard, along with his camera. I was driving and it was hard to see in the heavy rain, but I spun the boat around and made him out in the water. I could see his camera bobbing along, slowly sinking, and him swimming behind trying to get a hold of it.

'Mate, forget the fucking camera get in the boat!' I yelled. 'Leave it, get in the boat now!'

He was egg-beating in the water to keep his head up, basically inviting a crocodile to eat him.

'You'll be gone in a minute!' Mick shouted out and flung his hand over the edge of the boat. The cameraman hesitated and looked back at his device, then paddled over and Mick pulled him in. He was in shock, we all were.

'That's a $100,000 camera,' he said to me.

'Oh well, we've got another one at camp. You're lucky to be alive – who cares about the camera.'

No one spoke for the rest of the ride back to camp.

•

'Crocodile or no crocodile? Crocodile or no crocodile?' I asked the boys as we made our way back to the trap the next morning.

'Crocodile,' Ben said.

Everyone seemed optimistic, but I was uncertain.

To minimise our sounds and presence in the river we went upstream on the bank by foot until we got to a vista point in a tree. I climbed halfway up.

'I'll see if the trap has been activated. Chuck us the binoculars, Chris; it looks like the door has gone down.' I was optimistic for a moment. 'We're going to have to go and check it out.'

We took our boat from the bridge to the island and me and a few others walked cautiously towards the trap door.

'Wow, wow, just go steady, mate! Bait's gone and no croc,' Mick yelled out to me from the boat.

'Yeah, I can see that's a problem.' I climbed over and checked out the tracks. There was a large claw print and a biggish slide mark.

'It's a decent-sized croc, so how the hell did it get out?' Ben asked.

'The door is down and the bait is gone and . . . where's your knife, mate?' Mick asked me. I'd used my knife in part of the trigger mechanism I'd set in the trap, but now it was nowhere to be seen.

'Shit, the croc nicked my best bowie knife!' I exclaimed. 'Very cheeky. It looks like he's managed to wedge himself out through the bamboo panel on the bottom here.'

The panel closest to the ground was bent upwards. The trap clearly needed fortification but options were pretty limited in the Congo.

We spent the next few days sourcing new bits and pieces for it, but the best we could do was use sheets of chicken wire and hessian. We patched up the trap and reset it with new bait. Every day for the next two weeks was like groundhog day – head out in the morning, check the traps and swap out the cameras, then go back to the village for the afternoon. There were no crocs to be seen, they'd become uninterested. When it's wet, crocs often move out onto high ground trying to find food, so they're not in the main streams. I was frustrated because I knew if we had come in dry season we would have caught the croc in the first couple of days, but the heavy rain and water was making it almost impossible.

We brought a heap of soccer balls with us, so we spent our downtime in the afternoon playing with the kids and sharing stories with the locals around the campfire at night. Nights in the Congo were beautiful. No commercial lights, no interference – everything was pitch black with millions of stars that made the sky glow.

•

We had three days left in the Congo and had no croc to show for our month of hard work. Mick and I were spending our time scoping out the banks of the river right next to the village, working out the best place to build a caged wash bay and swimming area for the locals. It wouldn't last forever, but it was better than nothing.

I was walking along the bank with Mick a little way behind, when I heard rustling in the grass. I pushed through to a small clearing and saw a croc tangled up in rope, death-rolling around and causing a commotion.

'Oi, Mick!' I shouted. 'Come here quick and give me a hand to catch this croc while it's trapped.'

'Roger!' Mick called back.

The croc had obviously swallowed the bait from our trap with the rope still attached to it, and then got caught up in a tree on the bank. Just as Mick pushed through the clearing, the croc broke the rope around the tree and took off back into the water.

'Damn! He's gone. He was big but I don't think it was our fella!' I said.

'Hey, Matty, check this out,' Mick said from behind me. He leant down and picked something up. 'It's your knife, mate. The croc didn't fancy eating it.'

I couldn't believe it. We were kilometres from the island and a crocodile had returned my knife to me! That was the last thing I expected.

'Clever bloody crocs around here,' Mick remarked, and I had a good laugh. I was stoked.

Our last day in the Congo was full of mixed emotions. I felt like I'd failed Chris and Ben and let down the locals. I knew if the weather had been dry it would have been a different story, but I couldn't help but beat myself up.

All of us went on the boat to check the trap on the last day, and Pete, one of Hendri's friends, along with a local scientist, came with us. We were planning to take down the trap but, unexpectedly, we were greeted with action: two crocs throwing their weight around.

'There's a croc, oh shit! There's two! Game on, guys, here we go!' I launched out of the boat and jumped straight onto the trap's rails. There was a whole lot of yelling and commotion to follow.

'Mick, give me two ropes!' The crocs were thrashing around big time.

Ben passed me some rope.

'No, not that shit! Small rope, small rope!'

'Is there any other rope?' Mick asked the boys in the boat.

Before Mick could say anything else I yelled over everyone, 'Yes, there's other rope! Come on, let's get it!'

This was no time for messing around. I was worried the trap wouldn't hold the crocs for much longer.

'I want to secure the bigger croc first, then I'll go in and get the other one.' I climbed in on the inside of the cage and positioned myself to get a head rope over the croc.

'Watch yourself, man,' I heard Ben say as I jumped off the railing into the muddy, slushy water of the trap, pulling the head rope tight.

I handed the rope through to the guys. 'Secure this croc, give the rope some slack, and now pull!' I told them.

'I got him, I got him!' Chris and Ben held tightly on the other side of the railing. One down, one to go.

But the next croc was not giving in. I was moving around, making sure the tail of the first croc didn't whip me and the mouth of the second croc didn't nip me. Tension was high. I got into position and looped the head rope into place on my first go. The croc was secured.

'Ben and Chris, do you boys want to jump in with me?' I asked.

I figured it would help them face their fear. They looked anxious but they didn't hesitate and got in. I guided them through what to do. They worked the ropes and helped me put hessian over the crocs' eyes and tape up their mouths.

'In comparison to the head you guys saw on the croc that took Hendri, what are these guys like?' I asked.

'Yeah, I mean, they're definitely huge animals but it's not the one. The head isn't as massive,' Chris said.

I had a feeling it wasn't – these were a bit over 12 foot and from all accounts and the footage we saw on the first day, the big fella we were after was at least 16 foot.

'Okay, well, we should let these ones go then,' I said.

'But I'm concerned about this one,' Ben said, gesturing to the larger one. 'There's all those kids playing in the wash bay up stream. Can't we relocate it? This one, at least?" He didn't want me to let them go.

Mick cut through with reason, like he always does. 'Look, we came here with a particular goal, to catch a killer crocodile – we haven't seen a killer croc in person, we haven't caught a killer croc, so we're not just going to relocate one of these crocs and say close enough is good enough.'

Mick was right. The reality was that these crocs hadn't eaten people and there were hundreds more like these guys, so it wouldn't make a difference even if we did relocate them to a wildlife park. I called over the scientist who had come with us. I explained that I was going to mark the crocodile and asked him to record the markings for future tracking and reference.

Metal clip-on tags, like cattle tags, can be punched through a croc's tail scute (bony plate) but most of the time they get ripped out, so I tend not to use them. My preference is cutting the crocodile's scutes. If scutes are cut off at the base with a very sharp blade, then the marks are permanent and the scute heals without trouble. The scute measuring and identification system is a bit confusing but once you do it a few times it's simple. The point between the double row and single row of tail scutes is considered to be zero. Some people never cut these three scutes, so your starting point is always present. Counting down the tail from this point, the single scutes represent hundreds. The double scutes represent tens on the croc's left side and single numbers on the right. So you can create a unique number for any crocodile. (The last few single scutes should not be cut off, because crocs often lose their tail tips in territorial battles.) Using this numbering system, I cut off three scutes (100, 30 and 7) giving the croc the ID number of 137. The scientist wrote this ID number down along with a description of the croc. He was stoked; it was a good system for him to learn, especially because he worked a lot with crocodiles in the Congo.

'Okay, fellas, that's it, I guess,' I told everyone. 'Let's pack up this trap and use the gear to reinforce the wash bay barrier some more.'

It was the first time in my life I hadn't caught the croc I was after. I was so unsatisfied.

We said our goodbyes to the locals the very next morning and made our way home to Australia. I got straight back into egg collecting and thought about that bloody croc every night. It drove me nuts. I tried to get Nat Geo to fund Mick and me to go back in the dry season, but the ship had sailed. Chris and Ben returned to the village six months later and helped build and open the big new well in the town. I was glad to hear that we had made some sort of a difference in the community.

In November 2012, I got a call from our fixer telling me the croc had been caught and killed. I was devastated. Apparently it was spotted in the river while the military were around. They stood up on the bridge and opened fire on the water, then two days later the croc rose to the surface. It measured 16.1 feet and the locals feasted on it for weeks. Its fate made me feel sick. I know it was a man-eater, but it didn't deserve a gruesome death. It should have gone to a park, keeping both people and the crocodile safe. Still, I want to go back to the Congo again one day and see if life has improved in the village since the big fella got caught.

6
Unparalleled wildlife

From cocaine hippos in Bogotá to king cobras in Borneo, I had a pocket full of cash and was ready to make my mark on the world with *Outback Wrangler*. Pulling together season one of the TV show was pretty nerve-racking. It was my first time working on a big production and there were so many unknowns. The plan was to head to Bogotá, Colombia and Borneo to film two international shows and do two within Australia.

A fair swag of an entire floor of our production company's office in Sydney was taken over by people solely responsible for the show's preproduction. We had researchers, accountants, lawyers and assistants for assistants. I was a little frustrated because I'd recently requested a Cineflex high-definition camera system, which was fundamental to filming, but my request was shut down due to budget cuts. I can't throw stones because I've overemployed people in my own businesses before, but my hopes and dreams were tied up in the success of the first season and I wasn't going to let it be a flop. Although without the company there wouldn't have been a show, and what was great about the big team were the film and TV uni students. They did a lot of the groundwork for the main producers, tracking down the details for all of the contacts on the ground.

In particular, they connected me with a guy named Carlos, a wildlife ranger based in Bogotá. He had good English and knew his stuff, and I spoke to him every couple of days in the lead-up to the trip. Carlos and the other local rangers needed my help with resolving a major human–animal conflict.

Colombian drug lord Pablo Escobar built a private zoo back in the early 1980s on his ranch *Hacienda Nápoles*, about halfway between Medellín and Bogotá. Most of the exotic animals housed there were transferred to other zoos around the world, but not the hippos. Nobody knew exactly how many there were but the local authorities estimated around 50 to 60. We were going to use confiscated drug money, which the government held in a community beneficiary, to fund an operation to catch, rehome and de-sex about 30 of the rogue hippos. The hippos were territorial and aggressive and had been left to roam around the surrounding communities as they pleased, so there was a high risk to the safety of the people living in the villages. There had been a couple of attempts by other people to fix the problem but no real progress had been made. We wanted to move the hippos into a large enclosure so that they were still protected, but away from people.

Unfortunately, we ran into a curveball two weeks before filming. The GFC hit hard and the US dollar plummeted. The only option was to cut a show. Bogotá was the most expensive and logistically challenging, so it was a no-brainer for the production company: the episode was scrapped. I was pissed off, but I knew there was nothing we could do about it, and I didn't have a spare half a mil lying around.

So all of our international efforts turned to Borneo, where there were saltwater crocodiles and lots of other animals in conflict with humans, due to industry and development. Similar to the Northern Territory, the crocs in Borneo had been protected since the 1980s, which had caused human and animal conflict to increase, and the local rangers were looking for fair and peaceful solutions. My main focus was to train the wildlife rangers in catching and relocating saltwater crocodiles.

I was also going to provide support for the work with the local orangutans, elephants and snakes, all of which were being impacted by palm oil plantations. Malaysia, along with Indonesia, produces more than 80 per cent of the world's supply of palm oil. People call it the golden crop because it has lifted poor farmers out of poverty, but at a devastating cost to the environment. Over 90 per cent of orangutan habitat has been destroyed in the last 20 years, in what the United Nations calls a 'conservation emergency'. The more I learnt about it the sooner I wanted to get over to Borneo to film the show and spread the word about the horrific demise of the environment and its animals.

I was excited to check it all out, but I wasn't excited about what seemed like a cast of thousands that were heading over with me. I had just been in Australia filming two of the other *Outback Wrangler* episodes alongside the large team in Sydney, and the ground team in Borneo was just as big. There were risk-assessment people, medics, assistants, a producer, a researcher, a sound guy, a cameraman and a second cameraman. I knew all we needed was a soundy, producer and my two cameramen, that's it, but I went along with it nonetheless.

We landed in Kota Kinabalu – or KK, as it's commonly called – the state capital of Sabah, Malaysia. A convoy of 1980s Toyota Camry taxis with patchy, faded paint jobs pulled up to the rank and we jumped in. My car was filled with fluffy pink dice, eccentric bobbing figurines and other trinkets blu-tacked to the dashboard. The cab driver was friendly, a reflection of everyone else I met in Malaysia. We went straight to our hotel, passing through streets clogged with traffic, and bustling markets and people buzzing around everywhere. The city was alive. But as we pulled up to our accommodation I became enraged: it was a five-star hotel! We were in Malaysia to shoot a remote grassroots doco on a limited budget, and the production company had booked what I was sure was the most expensive hotel in town.

'Jesus Christ,' I said, as we got out of the cab.

'I know, it's just incredible, isn't it?!' the producer replied eagerly.

'Incredibly expensive,' I said back, sarcastically.

I dumped my bags in the hotel room and met up with Simon, our British fixer, on the ground, and we all headed to Lok Kawi Wildlife Park, a rescue park run by the Sabah Wildlife Rangers.

The Sabah Wildlife rangers' team leaders, JB and Dr Zen, were a lot savvier than I'd anticipated but their team was still very raw. JB told me about the poaching and loss of habitat, which had led to the pygmy elephant becoming gravely endangered; another sad example of humans and animals in conflict.

They asked me: 'Mr Matt, do you want to meet our latest rescue animal? She's just a baby. Her mum was shot by palm oil farmers.'

I was honoured and happily accepted the offer. One of the most memorable moments in my life was the time I spent with this cute cuddly girl. She was only 12 months old and weighed in at about 300 kilos. She was friendly and playful and just wanted affection. Her eyes were so innocent and kind and she deserved to be with her mother, but her mother had been killed.

Elephants know no better; they are so used to walking through the jungle looking for a feed, and now palm oil plants are the only option. And when they eat the hearts of the plants, the farmers just aim and shoot. The local wildlife team was working on creating rainforest corridors from one jungle to the next, laid out in between the palm oil plantations so the elephants can access the environments they need to survive. It's far from ideal but it's something, because the palm oil industry isn't slowing down, no matter how much backlash it receives. There is a lot of money tied up with people getting richer, and that greed is overcoming the love and need to protect our most valuable commodity – the environment.

I left the park with a heavy heart and travelled to a nearby croc enclosure I'd heard about just for a stickybeak, as the Malaysian saltwater crocodile or *buaya air masin* is identical to our crocs in Oz. Regrettably, the park stank like shit and the crocs were living in crappy conditions, so I made sure not to send any crocs I caught back to that facility.

After getting our feet on the ground in KK, it was time to pack up our gear and hit the road. On the way back to our stupidly lavish hotel I asked the cab driver to stop at the local market. I'd read a sign at the front of our hotel saying DURIAN STRICTLY BANNED BEYOND THIS POINT! I thought the durian was some sort of weapon, but when I asked JB at the wildlife park he said, 'Very, very stinky fruit like farts. Very popular but very bad.' I was intrigued and wanted to see if JB was right.

For those of you who haven't tried one: don't. The smell was so pungent that I gagged before taking a bite, but I blocked my nose and hooked into it – the mushy, slimy fruit squirmed around my mouth. I tried to swallow it but it was too much, I spat it out and the local ladies lost it laughing behind me. My orange-juice chaser didn't even disguise the taste.

I was happy to never see or smell the fruit ever again. After I got home to Australia, I remember reading food writer Richard Sterling's take on the fruit: 'Its odour is best described as . . . turpentine and onions, garnished with a gym sock.' I couldn't have said it better myself.

JB and the wildlife rescue team convoyed a couple of large trucks to Sepilok, a town about eight hours' drive from KK, while the crew and I flew there and met them at the other end. We landed at Sandakan Airport and drove the short distance to Sepilok, where we packed the truck with steel and equipment.

JB took me to meet his wife, who ran Sepilok Orangutan Rehabilitation Centre where around 80 orphaned orangutans live freely in the 43-square-kilometre reserve. Orangutan mothers are killed so poachers can take the babies to sell them illegally. Orangutans are also killed if they are found on the palm-oil plantations. I sat around the table with JB and his wife and talked about the orangutan program and the work we were about to do with the local animals. As we chatted, the orangutans swung around in the jungle behind us. It was beautiful to watch.

I held one fragile little female who hugged me like I was her dad.

'What's her story?' I asked. I wasn't expecting to hear what I did.

'We pulled her out of a brothel last week. She was used illegally as a play toy for entertainment and sex. This is very common,' JB said.

I was outraged. How could someone be so sick?

'At the end of our trip I'd like to come through here and do some filming with you all, so I can take your work and stories back to Australia to help raise money for you, if that's okay?' I asked.

JB's wife was stoked, but I felt it was the least I could do.

•

We were on the road again, headed for our main destination, Kinabatangan. All the shanties along the road caught my attention. I saw mothers feeding their newborns on the dirt ground outside their homes made of tin and salvaged wood planks, while kids were playing on dumpsites nearby. We'd just come from an opulent hotel and now we were amid poverty – Malaysia was a place of both hope and despair. We came up onto a ridgeline and looked out. Standing tall in the near distance was a bare hill. On one side of it were palm-oil plantations and on the other side was cleared rainforest. There was a solitary tree left on the top of the hill, and sitting beneath it was one lonesome orangutan. The scene spoke volumes about the environmental crisis sweeping not just Malaysia but the world. Everyone was saddened by the sight.

•

'I need a goat, pig or cow – anything, really,' I said to JB later that day. 'Just some sort of meat that I can use to bait all of our traps. I'd like to get an animal that's good for us to eat too.'

The rangers were excited because most of their meals were rice and veggies and, if they were lucky, sometimes fish, but meat was a luxury.

'Oh, very good, very good, of course, Mr Matt,' JB replied. He took us to a local market along the way where I bought a pig.

'That's 1200 ringgit, sir,' the young man said to me.

'Holy hell, I can see why you mob don't eat meat around here!' I was so used to catching as many wild pigs as I wanted back home for nothing, I converted the currency in my head and it was about 600 Australian dollars, which made a dent in my wallet, that's for sure.

I cut up the pig there and then, bagging it up and giving the ribs to the rangers, their grins were quite literally from ear to ear.

We left our cars next to a jetty and were picked up by boat and taken to our resort, Proboscis Lodge Bukit Melapi, located right on the Kinabatangan River. The river is the second longest in Malaysia, measuring about 560 kilometres long. It flows through Borneo's forests, rising from the mountains of southwest Sabah and running into the Sulu Sea. The river is home to ten species of primate as well as crocodiles, elephants, snakes, leopards and sun bears. I'm told there are also over 200 bird species. The forests along the river have been subject to widespread deforestation and poaching. JB and his team established the Kinabatangan Wildlife Sanctuary in 2005 as a response to the culling of forests and animals in the area.

•

The film crew and I checked in to the Balinese-style resort, then I grabbed a pillow and sheet from my room and headed straight back out the door.

'Where are you going, Matty?' Ash, my good mate and cameraman, asked, when he saw me heading off.

'I'm not staying here with this circus,' I told him. 'I want to earn the trust and respect of the rangers, so I'll go camp up the river where they are.'

'Fair enough, mate,' Ash replied.

I couldn't stay in a flash hotel and only be with the rangers when the cameras were rolling – what a joke. I taxied along the river to the rangers' accommodation. The river was long and wide and very muddy. All of the logging that was happening upstream meant there was nothing protecting the soil, and the big rains had caused erosion.

The wildlife team were surprised to see me. I found myself a spare room to put my gear in and offered to help the lads fix a leak in the toilet. I was almost done when the hose burst, squirting water all over me. Everyone paused in nervous silence to see my reaction. I burst out laughing and I could see the relief spread across their faces; they were trying to work out what sort of bloke I was.

The local village, located about 10 minutes away, was the closest street market to us, so JB and I went for a gander to get some extra grub to go with our rib dinner. I'd been to the amazing street markets in Bangkok before, but these markets were a lot less regulated. I came across *Larb Leuat Neua* – raw beef with uncooked blood, *Mok Huak* – developing tadpoles, and *Takatan* – grasshoppers. And as for refrigeration, well, there wasn't any. The flies fancied the fish and raw meat section, which I tactfully directed JB away from.

'JB, how about we just get some rice, veggies and lots of chilli for tonight,' I suggested. 'I love chilli.'

Thankfully, he agreed. 'Okay, Mr Matt.'

I figured I'd drown all my feeds with chilli to flush my system and avoid any food poisoning. My plan worked out well: even though I had bad gas the whole trip, I was the only person out of the entire crew who didn't fall victim to any food-related illnesses, even when the rest of the guys stayed at the fancy hotel.

A cold shower freshened me up after the market and I was outside talking through the next day's plan with JB when I started sneezing profusely and my eyes began to water.

'It's dinnertime now, the girls are cooking,' JB added with a big smile.

I was sitting downwind from the open communal kitchen and my senses were overtaken by the strong and powerful smells of chilli and other spices. The aroma was livening up the air and I became hungry all of a sudden. When the food came we all ate and chatted, and the warmth of the local people soaked through me. I felt at home.

•

One of the main things I wanted to do for the rangers while I was in Borneo was build them crocodile traps similar to the ones we used in the Territory. Our traps are light, collapsible and easy to transport. The ranger team were doing all of their work with these ginormous heavy steel traps, which took half a day to set up with trucks, machinery and a lot of manpower. The traps weren't effective or efficient, but I wanted to check them out first-up.

The rangers and I hit the road at first light. We met up with Ash and the soundy, and drove for one-and-a-half hours to the local palm-oil plantation to set up four crocodile traps along the river. One of the nearby landowners came over to JB and me and pleaded with us to find a large lizard that was eating his wife's kittens.

'Please catch the lizard. It's seven feet long and has eaten three of our kittens and we only have a couple of them left.' His wife and kids came out of the house and pleaded with me too, tears rolling down their cheeks. I was a croc-catcher not a kitten-saver, but I promised them I would do what I could.

As we walked away I said to JB, 'I will track down that lizard for them.' He brushed it off and laughed. 'Good luck! We have tried everything, but it always gets away.'

We had a backhoe loader and a large crane helping us get the traps into position. Back home it takes 15 minutes to set up a trap, but this took just over an hour for each one. It was a huge operation and there was no helicopter to help out, either. It was mentally draining more than physically exhausting because it dragged on and on. Finally we successfully set the traps and booted home.

Our little film crew were in the lead car and the rangers were following in file. I turned a bend and slammed on the brakes. There, lying across the road, was the biggest wild snake I've ever seen, a Burmese reticulated python. I was ecstatic. I had heard so much about the snakes of Borneo and was dying to work with one.

The Borneo rainforest is one of the oldest on Earth – it's been around for over 140 million years, so the animals have had plenty of time to develop. During the last ice age, land bridges linked Borneo to the mainland so species were able to migrate over to Borneo, leaving the island with an astounding array of animals. The snakes are particularly diverse. There are said to be about 150 species on the island and a lot of them are man-eaters.

I jumped out of the car to get a closer look at the python. It was about 16 feet long, with the girth of an AFL footy. It was a striking army-camo colour with a rainbow reflection across its back. *It must have just had a feed*, I thought to myself, because it wasn't moving. I stepped in to grab it by the tail and it bucked around with its mouth open.

'Wow! It's a bit spirited,' I called out.

Ash and the soundy were getting in position to film me. But after a few more attempts and a few more retaliations, I wasn't having any luck.

'"Not going to move" my arse. This thing is aggressive!' I called out again. I grabbed the soundy's boom stick and managed to pin the snake's head to the ground and picked it up.

'You need a hand?' JB and the boys had arrived and were out of their car, sounding very concerned for my safety. The snake had managed to wrap itself around my body like fairy lights around a Christmas tree, squeezing my chest and legs. I was holding its head, with its row of razor-sharp needle-like teeth moving about, wanting to lock on. Its head was the size of my hand. JB and the female vet nurse jumped in and helped me to unravel the snake while I stood there with a shit-heap grin on my face.

'Now that was cool,' I said.

'You're crazy, Mr Matt!' JB said, laughing.

'Hold on to the tail there and help me get this guy into a bag. I can move him somewhere else and away from the road tomorrow,' I said.

I had already seen monitor lizards and snakes as road kill, but they didn't last long around here. The locals were quick to collect any kill for their tucker.

•

Day three was trap-building day. Luckily, I had brought some gear from home in my duffel bag – battery-operated drills, grinders, a tool kit and other bits and bobs. I was welding away in the morning sun. I didn't have a mask, but I was making do and getting the job done nonetheless. I wanted to build four collapsible traps to leave with the team.

'Matt, Matt, Matt!' JB's call interrupted me as he came

running into the workshop area. 'King cobra, big deadly king cobra near our camp, can you help?!'

Two snakes in less than 24 hours? I couldn't believe my luck.

'Awesome. Ask one of the lads to run up and get Ash and the crew to film.'

Pumping with adrenaline, I followed JB to the car and we made our way to the nearby picnic park, a popular place for tourists and a less-than-ideal place for a venomous snake. We waited for the crew to catch up, then ventured into the little patch of jungle.

I have handled a lot of snakes in my time, and to me a snake is a snake, so I didn't think much different of a king cobra. I knew its toxin was deadly, but I still thought I'd manage just fine.

Boy, was I wrong. The snake was 11 feet long and it took me all of five seconds to work out it had one hell of a striking distance, as I moved straight in on it and it launched at me from five feet away.

'Ah, shit!' I exclaimed. 'This is going to make my life a little trickier.'

I was nervous and excited at the same time. It was a spur-of-the-moment catch, so there was no evacuation plan or antivenom available. If I was bitten, it would be an instant death.

After running around the jungle for a while, quite literally playing chasey with the snake, I was tiring out, and thinking, *Matt, what the hell have you got yourself into here?*

The wildlife team were standing back, taking it all in. They usually used baited traps and carefully planned a capture, so they were a little shell-shocked to see this foreign white man diving in around a king cobra.

After about half an hour of toing and froing, I realised the situation wasn't getting any better and was still thinking through the best way of getting this snake into a bag. I was in the middle of a face-off with a highly aggressive snake, trying to compose my thoughts, sweat pouring down my brow and panting like no one's business.

All of a sudden, I heard someone behind me. 'Stop, stop, stop! Stop this, Matt, and stop filming, Ash! We're not doing this as part of the show.' It was our producer, sounding like a nagging old teacher.

I paused for a second, focusing in on the snake and, without losing eye contact with it, yelled back: 'Listen here! YOU need to be quiet and go back to the car! It is not your place to advise me of what I can and can't do on my own fucking show and now is NOT the time!'

'But we don't have antivenom! This isn't in my risk assessment policy. I'll get sued if anything happens,' she shouted at me.

'Well, why don't you take your shitty risk assessment all the way to the car and back to Australia, because if you hang around here I WILL get killed. Now piss off!'

It was dead silent. No one said a word, and I saw her storm off to the car in my periphery. *Thank God for that*, I thought. I was furious – like hell was I going to stop filming. I pride myself on the content of *Outback Wrangler* being authentic and unscripted – that's what makes the show so unique, and my battle with the snake was as raw and real as it gets.

'JB, you got any tongs in your car?' I shouted. 'This bamboo stick isn't cutting it.'

'One moment!' I heard someone run off and return a couple of minutes later. I was expecting proper snake tongs at least a couple of metres long, but JB passed over what looked like a standard set of barbecue tongs.

'Mate, you hold onto those. I want you to grab the snake by its tail and I'll get him with my hands behind its neck. One, two, three, go!'

We launched in. The timing was perfect but shit, did the snake go ballistic, wrapping itself around my hand, trying to work its fang into my thumb. The trick with snakes is to not hesitate and be as precise as possible, handling them with the right amount of pressure. You need to hold the head firm, otherwise those two big fangs will connect with your skin.

The other wildlife boys brought over a bag and I dropped it in, making sure I kept my hands well clear, and tied the bag up as quickly as possible.

Phew, what a relief. I'd got the job done.

Well, almost . . .

'I am wondering, Mr Matt, only if you don't mind, can we take this snake to the clearing and let it out of the bag again, and you can take us through step by step what you did so we can learn this method without big tongs and traps?' JB asked.

I was completely wrecked and all I wanted to do was clock off for the day but he was so hopeful, and I wanted to help him and his team out.

'Yeah, I'd love to, mate,' I said.

Off we went and out came the snake again. I talked them through how to minimise stress for the animal, how to tell when a snake is about to strike, and how to hold onto the tail without it swinging around. The more we worked with the snake the quieter it got, and the rangers learnt that once a snake realises that you don't want to hurt it, it calms down completely.

By the end of the afternoon, I could hold the snake just under the belly without even having to grip its head. The rangers were in awe. I took the two snakes back to my room in separate bags and kept them next to my bed ready to release the next day, up the river, away from human activity.

•

I spent every spare minute I had in between filming making harpoons and traps. I'd burnt out the rangers in the first few days – I had them cutting steel, welding and grinding in the blistering heat. On the fourth day, the team had the day off, so I hopped in the boat and went to the hotel to see if any of the TV crew was free to lend a hand. Walking through the lush gardens of the resort I could hear bongo drums playing. I walked up the stairs to the entertaining area, expecting to see a traditional ceremony taking place. My jaw dropped.

'Oh, get off it,' I said under my breath. There, in the main compound next to the pool, was the assistant producer, playing bongo drums and surrounded by most of the crew, who were throwing back cocktails at 10 o'clock in the morning. The drum playing stopped as I approached, and everyone turned to me as if they had all seen a ghost. Dead silence.

'Oh, hey, Matt,' our researcher said, in a guilt-drenched voice.

'Where are the others?' I barked.

'Err . . . um, I think Ash is editing footage in his room and . . . the others might be sleeping?' the researcher said.

'You're kidding me! Jesus Christ, you're all useless. I'm working my arse off out here trying to make this show work and you guys are back here chewing up money, sinking piss, doing sweet FA! You're a pack of lazy leeches. I'm calling the production company and sending you home. There are too many hangers-on here and I'm sick of it!'

I feel shitty when I yell, and I keep my cool most of the time but I really was at wit's end. I stormed over to Ash's room where I found him downloading footage, and together we called the production company and got the go-ahead to send a bit of the deadweight home. A few of them packed their bags and left the very next morning. They hated my guts and I thought theirs stank pretty bad too.

•

Dr Zen appeared in the workshop early the next working.

'Sorry to interrupt, Mr Matt, but our spotters have confirmed a croc in one of our large traps in the palm-oil plantation.'

Dr Zen had already been sent the footage caught on the motion-sensor cameras, so we had a quick look to see what we were up against. For three days, the only action was from a big water monitor, the same lizard responsible for nicking the kittens. It would swim into the trap, set it off by eating the bait, and swim away through one of the gaps. These traps weren't like the cage traps we used back home, they had gaps big enough for the little sucker to get out. We all laughed as we watched this cheeky mongrel have a field day until we eventually saw our croc move in and get caught.

'Bingo!' I cried. 'That's our guy! Let's go, fellas!'

JB and the rangers usually relocated the croc in the same trap that the animal got caught in. Logistically, it's a nightmare, and doing it like that isn't good for the croc. It normally ends up with skin lacerations from being bumped around. So I was there to show the rangers how to safely remove it from the trap, tie it up and move it out in the open.

The team were keen to learn, and listened intently to what I had to say. 'First thing's first is getting the rope over the croc's snout while it's in the cage. Then get him up and away from the water. Pressure on the rope is a must. If he tries to run, hold the pressure and we stay together. No one gets in its way, okay?'

'Gotcha, Matt,' JB said, and a resounding chorus of *okay*

followed from the rest of the 12 rangers in the team. We were good to go.

Busting out of the trap, the 13-foot croc was as feisty as anything, putting up a colossal fight.

'Wait, wait, don't pull, let him roll! Let him tire himself out,' I instructed, guiding the team through the fundamentals of croc-handling.

The rangers were sporadically yelling out things in English, which added to the intensity of the situation. The croc growled, snorted and death-rolled up the bank, so I went in and jumped on it, securing it with the usuals – hessian, gaffer tape and rope.

'I can almost guarantee this is a male, but let's see if we can find the penis, fellas.' Everyone looked at me, mystified.

Generally speaking, males have thicker tail bases and are stronger in build. And this one looked a little too big to be a female, as girls never get bigger than 12 or so feet. But, unless you know a croc's age, it's virtually impossible to determine their sex without inspecting their bits.

Crocs have internal sex organs, which are housed inside a small slit below its belly, towards the tail. You have to insert your finger into the slit and feel for the hard internal penis to work out if it's a male. It's a lot more straightforward when the crocs are mating because the male's penis extends out of the slit, making it visible.

I picked up the tail of the croc, found the slit, inserted my finger and confirmed it was a male. JB did the same so he could understand firsthand what I was talking about.

Showing this to the guys was one of the most valuable, if not the most valuable, lessons I taught them, because knowing the sex of crocodiles is critical when you're trying to manage population numbers.

Locals with motorbike helmets on, barefoot teenagers and even a couple of police officers came scattering down the banks to be involved. I felt like a giant amongst the five-foot-tall locals who were all gathering around, staking out a space alongside the croc's body to be a part of the action.

We had close to 50 fascinated onlookers now, and when it came time to move the croc, everyone wanted to lend a hand. Usually you need three to four blokes to move a 13-foot croc, but we'd ended up with at least 20 local volunteers carting out the 400-kilo animal. I kept hold of the croc's head, so if he shook it didn't knock any of them out.

We loaded the croc on the back of the truck and I sent my film crew on ahead, instructing them to grab the snakes from my room. They were to meet the rangers and me at the boat ramp near the tourist information centre where we'd launch off and take the animals to their final spot for release.

The day's comedy show kept coming. The rangers and I arrived, unloaded the croc and intended to carry it down the path to the boat ramp. What I didn't realise was that the path cut straight through the front doors of the information centre and out the other side. I couldn't believe it. This relocation was meant to be incognito and there we were carrying a croc bigger than two men put together right past picnic benches where people were eating lunch and taking holiday photos. *This is like a* Fawlty Towers *episode*, I thought to myself.

We pushed open the doors and were greeted by a small group of female trekkers who fell to the floor like they were taking part in a 'stop, drop and roll' fire drill. And fair enough, six blokes casually carrying a croc through the information centre was probably the last thing they expected to see. We just smiled and kept walking. (It made for a good story, though. The incident ended up on the front page of every newspaper around Malaysia with the headline LOCAL HERO JB AND HIS WILDLIFE TEAM RELOCATE BIG CROC FROM POPULAR SWIMMING HOLE with a picture of us trudging through the tourist centre.)

When you're filming, everything takes twice as long, with interviews and retakes. By the time we met up with the crew again, loaded the animals onto the boat and scoffed down some lunch, it was 2 p.m. and we'd only just set off along the river.

'We are going to move this croc up to the research station, where university students come to study Borneo wildlife,' JB told us.

'How long will that take?' Ash asked.

'About two hours,' JB and the vet nurse replied in unison.

The boat was comfortable enough for the journey, with a large centre console and a fair bit of room for the rangers and film crew. As we poked along the river, we could see the trees moving around us and the long-nosed proboscis monkeys dancing through the branches. Their honking calls echoed around us, and every now and then an orangutan showed itself in a clearing.

We stopped off after an hour and released the cranky cobra and reticulated python safely into an expansive area of jungle where they could roam around without being harmed or causing harm. Then up the Kinabatangan River we continued. We had to be constantly on the lookout for the logs that were all through the river from the deforestation. It was okay going while it was light because we had visibility, but we'd been on the river for at least six or seven hours when the sun began to set. It certainly wasn't a two-hour trip as promised. Every 30 minutes or so JB would say 'Not far now, not far now,' which lost its meaning after the third or fourth time.

The moment it got dark the driver dropped our speed significantly, and we putted along the river at a painful snail's pace. The croc got restless a couple of times, swiping me with his head and knocking our soundy to the ground with his tail. After what seemed like an eternity, we reached the research centre, where we discovered the real reason for our visit.

It wasn't just to relocate the crocodile. A group of university students studying zoology, crocodiles in particular, were staying at the centre. None of the students had ever caught, let alone *seen,* a crocodile, and they were studying them! I ended up having to do a lesson at 9 o'clock at night on crocodiles, before I showed them how to handle and release the animal correctly. It was now 10 p.m. and we'd been going since 6.30 a.m. I was wet with muddied water, my muscles ached and I could feel the skin coming off my prune feet. I was tired beyond belief.

Thick dew and fog set in as we headed back to the tourist centre, making it colder and even more unpleasant. The thought of the seven-hour journey ahead was tormenting me. I ended up on the deck covering myself with a stinking wet rag that I'd used to cover the croc's eyes. It's amazing – even when you're wet – that if your body warmth is there you can actually stay relatively snug, so I was trying to stay as warm as possible.

I dozed off for a while and woke up hoping to see the tourist centre, but . . . nothing. I looked over the side of the boat and then turned to Ash, who looked like he'd just woken up too.

'Mate, are we going downstream or upstream?'

'Only one way home, mate, and that's downstream,' Ash replied confidently.

I frowned. 'Are you sure?'

'Yes, I'm sure.'

I got my head lamp out and checked overboard again. 'I don't think we are, man.'

I stared closely at the flow of the river. The water was bubbling through the reeds and up against the bank in the wrong direction.

'I bet my left arm we're going back upstream!' I called out.

'Nah, mate, don't be silly. There is no way we could have turned around,' Ash said to me.

No one else agreed with me either, so the driver kept going.

'I guarantee you we are!' I insisted.

'No, no, we are going downstream,' JB chimed in.

I was bursting with frustration that no one was listening to me and I wasn't having any more of it. 'Just stop! Just stop now! Completely stop the boat and pull over to the bank and let's have a look,' I said.

This time, the driver listened. We stopped, and immediately started drifting backwards.

'Oh my god, we're going upstream! How long have we been going this way for?' I yelled out again.

Everyone looked at one another, puzzled. No one had any idea.

It turned out that we had somehow rotated around in the black of the night and travelled even further past the research centre. I couldn't believe the carelessness of the crew. I sat there for a moment while *What the hell were you thinking? Why wasn't anyone paying attention? What an absolute waste of time!* came and went from the tip of my tongue, restraining myself and my loose lips. No one said a word, everyone just sat there completely deflated. We turned around and drove home, finally arriving back to base at 6.30 a.m., just as the sun was rising. At that point even I needed some creature comforts, and traded in the staff quarters for a hotel room to sleep off the drowsiness.

It was the longest day of my life.

•

The first thing that comes to mind when you think of an elephant is an animal big in size, but Borneo elephants, also known as pygmy elephants, are neither gigantic nor aggressive. They stand between 7 to 10 feet in size and weigh between 3000 to 5000 kilos. They're very cute and I felt privileged to have had the opportunity to work so closely with them in the wild.

A couple of days after the boat incident, a report came through from JB's spotters that there were a few herds of elephants in the palm-oil plantation not far from where we caught the croc. If we didn't move them, they would be shot by workers there. Before the days of extensive plantations, pygmy elephants roamed around in herds of 40 or so. Nowadays you're lucky to see a herd of 10 because so many are killed by plantation workers.

The sad part about relocating them out of harm's way is that even though you're doing some good you're also splitting up the small families that are left. Six or seven is a standard number for a herd, but the rangers can only relocate two to three at a time, so by the time the rangers return to move the remaining elephants, they have already moved on to another part of the plantation and can't be found again. But still, the rangers would rather move two or three at a time than leave them in the plantation to get killed.

We drove out in a convoy of three trucks with big cages, four smaller vehicles, a front-end loader, a 30-tonne excavator and associated equipment, along with the full team of 16 rangers, some scientists and PhD students. It felt like a cast of thousands but, from what I understood, we would need as many hands as possible to move the elephants once we had them tied up because they are such solid animals.

'All right, when we get there I only want Matt and me on foot with the camera crew. Everyone else is to stay in the trucks until we need all hands on deck,' Dr Zen said across the radio to everyone. 'The elephants are usually pretty calm but can charge sometimes if startled, so we need to reduce our risk.'

He turned to me. 'Mr Matt, if the animal comes at you just run and get out of the way.' I heard him out but didn't agree with the running away part. Panicking and running usually draws more attention and reason for an animal to run you down.

We spotted the herd and snuck through the plantation with the film crew tracking closely behind us. Dr Zen singled out a cow and her calf along with a bull, then called in the rest of the team over the radio to move in behind. The elephants appeared to be a family unit, so he focused on keeping those three together for the relocation. He wanted to get the cow first because he knew that the calf would stay near her, and then he planned on moving quickly to the calf, and then the bull.

Dr Zen stopped, pulled out his little case of drugs and .50-calibre dart, and loaded the syringe with the immobilising drug. Once we got close enough to the elephants he released the dart, which was propelled from the gun with the help of compressed gas.

The dart hit the cow, administering the drugs. We thought all was going well but the bull must have heard us moving in behind them, because it turned back to face us and started to charge.

Holy shit, I thought.

The commotion caused the other herds to start stampeding around us. Everyone scattered and skidded behind the palm trees like panicked mice. There were some close calls with the camera crew when a couple of bulls started chasing the guys up the arse, but the elephants continued on, flapping their ears and trumpeting through the tall timber.

I'd been in situations similar to this many times before with a loose brumby during a muster, so, while everyone ran around like headless chooks, I just waited for the elephants to charge right at me and stepped behind a big tree at the very last minute. Then I sat back and watched the circus unfold for a bit. It was hysterical.

Dr Zen quickly loaded half of the next dose in another dart ready for the calf, as he didn't want her to run off and be without her mum. But the same bull we were trying to relocate turned back towards us and started charging again, and Dr Zen had no other choice than to let off the half-dose on the bull. That slowed him down for a moment while Dr Zen reloaded another half-dose, and then we lunged towards him and put another dart in him.

We had to be so careful with the second dart, because if you overdose an elephant it falls over and can't get back up on its feet. And if they're on their side for too long, the pressure on their lungs gets too much and they can drown in their own fluids.

They tried to move away but the bull had now been darted with its two half-doses, and the cow was really starting to slow as the drugs kicked in. Luckily for us, the calf just wanted to be with her mum, so she moved quietly alongside the other two. All three animals began to lag behind the rest of the herd and we could follow them easily, with their large tracks marking the ground. We pursued them, shadowed by the team of rangers, until the bull began to stumble.

'Okay, go!' Dr Zen called out, and the rangers swarmed the bull, attaching metal cuffs and chains to his legs and tying him to a tree to ensure he stayed upright. The moment the elephant was secured they administered the antidote, bringing him back to his senses.

'Oh no, look at this,' Dr Zen said from behind me.

There was a huge cyst, the size of a soccer ball, on the bull's arse. Dr Zen got out his scalpel and made a tiny incision right on the cyst's surface. The bull didn't even flinch. Out oozed buckets, and I mean *buckets*, of pus, followed by a bit of blood. It made me feel so sick to watch and I dry-retched at the smell of the open wound.

'There will be a bullet in here, Mr Matt.'

Dr Zen was right. Once the fluid was released, out came a little bronze bullet from a .22 shotgun, or something similar.

'Poor fella. Lucky he's still a little groggy,' I said.

All three elephants were now chained up, calm and ready to be moved into their pens for transportation. Timing and accuracy were critical, and JB, Dr Zen and their team had nailed it.

It took us a full day of mucking around and a hell of a lot of people to tie up and move the animals. Then torrential rain started pouring down. We couldn't move them any further towards the trucks in that weather, so we had to leave them tied up comfortably with a few of the wildlife carers camped out in the cars nearby to look after them.

There was massive rain that night, and over the next few days. We couldn't even make our way back out to the plantation, the rain was that heavy. I didn't want to do nothing, so I moved my workshop gear to the hotel and finished welding up all of my traps to leave with the rangers.

I walked out of my room on the morning that the rain stopped, and couldn't believe my eyes. There had been over a metre of rainfall and the river had risen to meet my doorstep, which was about four or five steps from the pathway that led down to the riverbank. It was nuts. Boats were floating past me like I was in a ground-floor apartment next to a water canal in Venice. A piece of driftwood bobbed by, followed closely by a 12-foot crocodile.

'G'day, mate,' I greeted it. 'Coming in for a visit?'

It had obviously smelt the pig bait I had lying around and was hoping for a feed. I waited for the croc to piss off along the river and made my way down the steps, finding myself touching the bottom submerged in water up to my waist.

JB came around with a little dinghy and picked me up from my doorstep. He couldn't have come at a better time.

'The elephants are okay, but the calf had to swim around for a bit because she couldn't touch the ground. There's a lot of water where they are too, so the relocation's going to be difficult,' JB said.

The truck drivers navigated the muddy roads into the plantation, backing themselves in as close to the animals as they could manage. We had a 25-tonne excavator that came in and lifted the pens off the backs of the trucks. It was a muddy shitfight but we managed to walk the elephants into the open pens with the aid of prongs, which JB gently prodded in behind their ears. After another drawn-out day we got them into the caged pens and the crane on the back of the truck, lifted them up and lowered them securely on the tray. I could see why relocations like this only happened once a week in *good* weather – it was one hell of a job.

I could see so many improvements that could be made and thought of lots of different ideas, but I kept my mouth shut. There's nothing worse than an outsider coming in and making suggestions that are good in theory but practically have zero likelihood of being achieved. It's not because they weren't good, but I knew I had a limited knowledge of how they could actually be put into practice in an environment with challenges and issues I wasn't overly familiar with.

It was a four-hour drive to the elephants' new home. The area of rainforest backed onto another plantation, but the thing was that this particular plantation was surrounded by an electric fence, so there was no way the elephants could become displaced. Essentially, they would be trapped in their own habitat with a river forming one boundary and an electric fence forming another. We turned off the electricity and flattened one area of fencing to get the trucks in and released the beautiful creatures. It was such a good feeling seeing them amble off happily together. We put the fence back up, turned the electricity on and made our way home. I wish we'd had even more machinery and manpower, so we could have relocated the herds together and kept families intact but at least we saved some lives. It was a good start.

•

The next story I am about to tell you involves the most dangerous experience of my life. How I didn't die on this particular day, I still don't know.

It was time for me to show JB and the team how we collect crocodile eggs back home. I explained to them that using helicopters and other machinery makes life a lot easier, and I decided to hire a chopper to demonstrate exactly what we do.

Four thousand dollars later, in flies a long-range-helicopter with a bloke I later named Captain Courageous (can you sense the sarcasm?). He flew in with a co-pilot, which was unnecessary, as well as a rope specialist.

I walked up to the co-pilot and shook his hand, then turned to the pilot to shake his.

'G'day, mate. I'm Matt, how ya going?'

He stood up straight, folded his arms and said in short, sharp syllables: 'You must call me Captain.'

'Righto, Captain,' I said back, turning to Ash with a half-smirk on my face, thinking, *Is this bloke for real?*

To top it off, he was wearing epaulettes (the shoulder badges worn by fixed-wing pilots), and his badges had four stripes each, the very top ranking available. That in itself was a joke to me. If you ever see a chopper pilot wearing epaulettes, well, they shouldn't be flying a chopper. Back in Australia if you're a chopper pilot you're just seen as a glorified ringer, a cowboy in the sky, but it was obviously different in Malaysia. I thought about it some more and realised it was probably quite a notable job for a lot of the locals, and perhaps that's how protocol was in their country so I respected his wishes.

The rope specialist was a great lad and showed me the ropes, quite literally. We obviously didn't have the double-hook sling set-up we used back in the Territory, so for some harebrained reason it was decided that abseiling down from the chopper was the best way into the nest. Why on earth we didn't just hook ourselves up while on the ground and sling in that way has got me fucked. But I do remember someone from the helicopter company suggesting we abseil from the chopper and me thinking, *Hell yeah, that'd fun. I can't do it in Australia so if it's legal here and they're going to sign it off, why not give it a crack!*

'Have you ever abseiled before, mate?' the rope specialist asked me.

Willow heading back to camp on the sling after a day's work collecting croc eggs on La Belle Station. Craig and Mick are on foot.

Age 25, egg-collecting on the Victoria River back when Jimmy and I were the 'two rascals'.

Flying the chopper over the nests at Arafura Swamp in Arnhem Land, NT.

One of the bigger crocs I caught on the Vic River back in 2004, when I was working on Moroak Station as a ringer.

The *Outback Wrangler* core team: Jono (r), Willow (c) and me. Here we are catching and relocating a handful of small female crocs on Elizabeth Downs Station.

An 18-foot monster crocodile caught during filming for season three of *Outback Wrangler*.

CAT

Above: Using an excavator to pull out another big crocodile, just one of the methods we used to get the crocs out of their pens at Wyndham Crocodile Farm.

Opposite: 17-foot croc Axel getting moved from Wyndham Crocodile Farm during the 'wild west' mass relocation. Today, he lives at Crocosaurus Cove in Darwin.

Below: Carrying the Devil to the back of the truck to join Axel.

The back of the truck, filled with hay and covered by shade sails, providing a comfortable spot for the Wyndham crocs.

Crossing the river in the Congo on the so called 'ferry' made up of canoes strapped together with a steel sheet laid across the top.

Chatting to the crew in the Congo, making jokes about the precarious river crossing we were about to make.

Mick and me in the Congo, admiring the incredibly straight wooden harpoon poles, handcrafted by the locals with only a small knife and some sandpaper.

Practising erecting the panel trap just outside Kabeya Maji to ensure we had everything we needed before we set the trap for real.

Our main camp set-up in Kabeya Maji, where we slept and ate around the fire most nights, sharing stories with one another.

Talking to camera while sitting on the back of the bigger of the two crocs that I caught while I was in the Congo.

The set-up of Outback Floatplane Adventures in the very early days of operation. We didn't even have a helipad so I had to land the chopper on the roof of *Cyclone Creek*.

Macca and me doggedly transporting the Polaris, ready for the first ever tour for Outback Floatplane Adventures.

Hanging out with my 17-foot pet croc Tripod in his pen at the back of the shack.

My three-legged scaly mate in all his glory, turning it on for the cameras.

Welding up the traps with one of the wildlife rangers in the workshop shed in Borneo.

Baiting and securing a cage trap in Borneo, showing two of the rangers how to activate the trapdoor.

Top left: The Burmese reticulated python I found lying across the road in Borneo.

Top right: Relocating the python and a crocodile upriver during the infamous boat trip that lasted until the next morning.

Right: 'Captain Courageous' flying me insanely high in the sky while I screamed and swore into oblivion.

JB and me connecting with the bull elephant we caught and relocated in the jungle.

Releasing the beautiful orangutans at the wildlife sanctuary.

Kaia and me just after we said our vows at our wedding in Dunsborough, WA.

Suited and booted with my closest mates on my wedding day – groomsmen from left to right: Mick, Clayton, Jono, Dhani and Jai.

Kaia and me on the Injidup cliffs, getting photos with the same chopper I landed on Rottnest Island in when we first met.

I was playing around with the abseil catch, trying to suss out how the rope fed through it. 'Yeah, yeah, sure have.'

It was a flat-out lie. I'd never abseiled before, let alone seen anyone do it.

'And you've done it out of a chopper before, yeah?'

'Yeah, mate, of course, heaps of times.'

The lie was expanding by the second. I had no idea what I was doing, but in life, I never say no to anything because I don't like opportunities passing me by. And I definitely didn't want this adventure to slip through my fingers. I just figured I'd say yes, then work it out quick-smart as we went along.

The rope guy briefed us on abseiling from the chopper, which was a little more complicated than I'd expected. We all went through the ins and outs of how JB and I were going to make our way down the rope and on and off the crocodile nests. I put a helmet on and had GoPro cameras strapped all over me to get footage for the show. I was ready to rock and roll.

'Who am I?' the pilot asked me as we were getting into the chopper.

I looked at him, confused.

'What is my name?' he asked me again.

I caught on to what he was saying. He was trying to reaffirm that I knew to call him Captain. This guy had to have tickets on himself.

'You're Captain Courageous,' I said back, joking around.

'No, just Captain,' he snapped back at me. 'You must call me Captain at all times. I am Captain, you are passenger.'

'Jesus Christ, here we go,' I said to Ash, who chuckled and hopped into the chopper. We'd agreed that he'd spend the day switching between the chopper and the support boat on the river to film, while JB and I taxied around in the chopper with the two pilots.

'Have fun with Captain, my man!' Ash called out sarcastically.

Before we headed out to the crocs, we decided to practise a bit. JB and I had our ropes hooked onto our harnesses at one end and underneath the chopper at the other end. I gave it a go first. I shimmied myself out of the helicopter door and onto the edge of the skid. While I was sitting there, leaning in towards the chopper, I made sure my rope wasn't tangled and then gently pushed myself off, swinging under the machine. I was relying on equipment and a system that was completely thrown together. If I had fallen from this height of 100 feet, I would have been in a pretty bad way. There were no testing or safety precautions taken, either; I'd just jimmied up a carabiner and was hanging on a 10-mm-thick rope that was linked to a pulley system I didn't know how to use. In hindsight, it's pretty ridiculous but I was so excited to give abseiling from the chopper a go that I didn't really think about it.

I punched off and pretty much zip-lined down this 100-foot rope, almost in freefall because I forgot how to pull on the mechanism.

I was ripping down as fast as anything, thinking, *Oh shit, gotta stop, gotta stop*. I jerked the rope just as I got to the end, and bounced back up.

'Right, I've got that part worked out now,' I said to myself, heart racing.

After the fifth test JB and I had it sorted and were feeling confident enough to get in on a croc nest so I could show him how to approach, open and clear a nest safely and efficiently.

Apart from the 'Higher, Captain', 'Lower, Captain', 'Please go this way, please go that way, Captain', which I had to say on repeat, I was really enjoying myself, and even though what I was doing was risky, I didn't feel like my life was ever really in danger.

But boy, was that about to change. JB and I had collected a couple of the nests and our slinging and abseiling in and out of the chopper and nests was going perfectly. JB explained to the pilot that there was a particular nest about a kilometre away that he wanted us to check out. Instead of climbing back into the helicopter for the journey, I stayed on the end of the line. This is no different to what we do in the Territory, but the pilot usually flies only 10 or so feet above the ground or trees to ferry us safely to the next location.

Without warning, I felt myself being lifted higher and higher into the air.

'Stop, Captain, stop! What are you doing?! Too high, Captain, too high!' I called out over my handheld radio.

I went from 100 feet to 200 feet and that figure was doubling and doubling as he flew higher and higher. I started shouting every single swearword under the sun, screaming and screaming at the stop of my lungs for him to fly lower but nothing was happening. My messages weren't getting relayed. He began doing a full flight circuit and was flying up in circles until he got to over 1000 feet. I was completely nauseous, anticipating the thin rope snapping at any minute.

This is it, I thought, picturing myself plummeting to my death.

I tried one more time at the top of my lungs 'STOP, YOU FUCKING IDIOT!' but it was lost in the wind and my voice was breaking I had worn it out completely from all the yelling.

At that point I stopped trying to communicate with Captain altogether and hung on for dear life, just hoping that by some miracle I would make it back to ground safely.

I eventually felt the chopper descending, bringing me in to land. My feet touched the ground near a nest, and I unhooked and sprinted into a clearing nearby, waving my hands wildly out of rage. The pilot came in to land next to me.

I have never felt rage like it in my life. I know this sounds terrible but to be honest I wanted to grab the pilot by the head and skull-drag that idiot out of the captain's seat and punch the shit out of him. Fuck, I was angry. But I held back, absolutely served it to him verbally and then waited until Ash and the rangers arrived by car to collect me. They'd been tracking our progress on the boat. Ash told me he could hear everything I was saying over *his* radio on the boat, but the pilot had obviously been tuned to another frequency. I have no idea what made him fly so high. No one in their right mind would do something like that, so I was happy to never see Captain Courageous and his stupid face ever again.

That night, Ash showed me a picture of me in the air, a tiny speck of a thing. You couldn't even make it out that I was a person, that's how high up I was. It took me a bit to wind down before getting to sleep, and the memory of that day still haunts me.

•

It was our last day with the rangers before heading home. We packed up, said our goodbyes and made our way back to the airport, taking a small detour past the orangutan sanctuary on the way.

'JB, let's just stop over in the swimming hole one more time on the way out and make sure there aren't any crocs in the traps,' I said.

As we came to the bridge my eyes lit up.

'The lizard, the bloody lizard, that's it!' I called. 'Stop the car, Ash! I'm getting out, come with me!'

I took off without shoes or a microphone, skidding down the banks and into the shallows. The lizard looked even bigger in real life; it was at least seven feet long and fat as anything. It scurried into the water when I arrived, and I traced its movement by watching the weeds waving around on the surface as it waded beneath. The bank was littered with fallen palm fronds, which were stabbing my bare feet with every step I took. It was agonising, but I wanted to get this kitten-eating lizard so badly. I took a big step forward, ready to leap on the lizard while it was in the water, then hesitated.

'Ah shit, I wonder if there's another big croc in here,' I called out.

Ash and our soundy were standing on the bank, trying to film. The soundy was stretching the arm of his boom mic as close to me as he could get it.

'Nah, Matty,' Ash called back. 'Go for it, mate, you'll be sweet!'

I listened to Ash and went in hard, landing right on top of the lizard and boy, did it kick up a fight. Its feet were as big as mine and its talons were otherworldly, larger than any claws I'd ever seen on a wedge-tailed eagle.

I pulled the lizard in as close to me as possible, and its back legs scrabbled up mine, ripping through my jeans on both legs and cutting my skin. It hurt, but I held on tight, and ran up the bank with the lizard and straight to JB. The smile on his face was priceless, and he just started laughing. 'Only you, Mr Matt, only you.'

I gave it to him and he passed it onto another ranger, who put it into a cage in the back of their little truck to release on their next trip to the rainforest.

There was no better way to finish off the trip than at the orangutan sanctuary with JB and his wife. They let me help with the release of two orphaned orangutans back into the wild. JB took one and the other, a two-year-old girl, jumped on me. She held onto me in a piggyback, just chilling as we walked through two-and-a-half kilometres of lush jungle to the release platform. It was a beautiful experience.

One of the handlers at the sanctuary came with us, and warned me about a dominant male orangutan that had been known to hang around where we were going to release the two orphans.

'He's a bully, and has a habit of pooing and throwing it at people,' the handler explained. 'Just keep an eye out for him, and don't make eye contact with him or any of the bigger animals the deeper we get into the jungle.'

I've seen footage of orangutans pulling people's limbs off before, so I didn't like the sound of coming face to face with this cranky male.

I walked my girl up the steps of the release platform where we would let her go.

Slap!

Something hit the side of my face. I looked around but couldn't see anything.

Slap! Something hit me again, and I looked down to see two banana peels at my feet.

'You okay, Matt?' JB asked.

'Yep, all good.'

'It's the big guy we were telling you about,' JB continued. 'Just ignore him, it will be okay.'

We carried on with the release and the two orphans swung out of our arms with ease. I've released lots of rehabilitated animals before and it's always an emotional experience. I'd only spent the short walk with my girl but

I bonded with her instantly. She took a tiny piece of my heart with her, that's for sure.

'Go well, girl,' I said as she finally disappeared into the distance.

JB and the handler stepped down the ladder first and I followed them, making my way to the ground. Unexpectedly, the shadow of a big orangutan appeared from above me, grabbing my arm with force. I froze.

'Matt, squat down. Kneel into a ball and don't look up,' I heard the handler say to me.

I sat on the ground for a few minutes, with JB and the handler squatting beside me. The orangutan prodded me a few times, putting his weight on my shoulder. After leaning on me for a good minute, he eventually let go, paused momentarily, then swung away.

'Okay, Matt, you need to stand up slowly, don't look back, and just walk away with us at a normal pace.'

I followed the handler's instructions and off we went, without any further problems. My heart was still pounding, thinking about what could have been.

'Well, that seems like a very fitting way to finish off a trip of a lifetime, full of every single possible wildlife encounter that most people can only dream of!' I said to JB and the team when we got back to the group and I told them the story.

I gave my hat, boots, jacket, belts and knives to JB as a thank-you present. Leaving him with my things was the least I could do, when he, Dr Zen and the team of rangers gave me experiences and memories I'll never forget.

7
My mate Tripod

CROCODILES INVADE FOOTY FIELD, TOURISTS WADE THROUGH CROCODILE-INFESTED WATERS, MONSTER CROC MAKES A MEAL OUT OF A KANGAROO and CROCODILE ATTACKS MAN are just some of the news headlines to come out of Daly River.

You get the picture. Daly River, located midway between Darwin and Katherine in the Northern Territory, has crocs – big ones, and lots of them. It's pretty fitting, then, that Tripod, my Instagram-famous 17-foot pet crocodile, called the Daly River home. It is where he was caught back in 1986 for causing havoc and trying to eat the local traditional owners, who were camped out along the river. Nick Robinson, a famous NT croc catcher, pulled a then-15-foot Tripod out of the main waterway with the help of a young Indigenous fella by the name of James Perry.

The story has it that when Nick asked James to help him bait the trap, the young fella took it upon himself to get the job done while Nick wasn't there. James got a horse leg, tied it over his shoulder and swam across the croc-infested Daly River to the other side of the bank, where he baited the trap. James emerged from the river completely unscathed and lived to tell the tale. The croc was caught that very same night James baited the trap, so when the croc was finally pulled out to be relocated, everyone named him 'James' and the story became a bit of a Territory legend. The croc had his front right leg torn off in a battle with another croc before he was caught on the Daly, and it was actually me who renamed him 'Tripod' when he ended up at my place years later. It's unfortunate for Tripod, but it means he is easier to work with because his mobility is pretty limited, and his remaining front leg doesn't do much for him either. Essentially, Tripod is part prehistoric monster, part immobilised slug. But there's no denying he'd still eat you in a heartbeat if you gave him the chance – slowness does not mean passiveness.

Tripod was moved to the NT Crocodile Park, where he was kept in the tourism section, wowing guests with his impressive size and presence. I started running my Outback tours in 2005 and, as part of the experience, I took guests through the park for a private feeding show with some of my favourite crocs, including Tripod. The tourism side of the park shut down in 2007 due to biosecurity restrictions. The facility was then converted into a fully functioning farm while Crocosaurus Cove, a crocodile tourism park, opened up in Darwin so tourists could still experience crocodiles up close. Many of the pens in the old facility were knocked down and opened up to create more spacious breeding facilities, and part and parcel of this was having to integrate the crocs who were once kept separately. Just like they do in the wild, the males immediately asserted their dominance over one another, and some pretty impressive fights broke out.

It was the middle of the breeding season, and a small number of crocs had hatched from uncollected eggs in the facility's new open areas, which comprised about 20 acres of expansive swampland. Jimmy and I got tasked with catching and relocating the little ones into smaller enclosures. Given that crocs are primarily nocturnal, we went in the dead of night, when they are most active out of the water so we could see them more clearly. We drove out in a ute on the lookout for crocs around two-foot in length. We intended to catch them, tape them up and put them in the back of the tray.

We reached the first large pond and the ute's headlights revealed well over 100 crocs, which if you can imagine, is a hell of a lot of crocs moving around in the one area. It's an amazing sight, even for someone like me who sees that sort of thing a lot. Some were partially submerged in the water, but most were stretching out along the banks.

We idled in the ute for a moment and then I spotted a little one about four metres from the water's edge. I hopped out of the truck with my net and started to creep up on it. I became more cautious the closer I got to the water, well aware of the big aggressive males lurking in there. I tiptoed up and scooped the first one into my net, no worries.

But as I walked back to the ute with it, it started calling out to its mum.

A croc's call sounds kind of like a cross between a duck's quack and a frog's croak. It's distinctive, and it's *loud*. This croc would not stop calling and it was getting louder.

'Shhhh,' I shushed it under my breath, and increased the speed of my powerwalk back to the ute, where Jimmy had already caught another little one.

'Their calls are going to attract some unwanted attention,' I said to him.

'You're telling me! I just had a gnarly female fly metres into the air to have a crack at me. She literally flew, mate, got completely airborne. I ain't ever seen nothing like it!' Jimmy was pretty wound up, and it did feel like we were asking for trouble.

There was another little one I saw near the bank that I wanted to collect before we called it a night. So I crept back down to the water and jumped on her from behind. She immediately started calling her parents for help and then, sure enough, out of the water came two big, angry females, making a beeline for me. Luckily, they emerged from the same direction, so I had a clear path to run the other way. They both chased me right up to the ute and I had to high-jump into the tray. Jimmy was already sitting in there, panting and sweating.

'I'm done with this, Matty,' he said. 'We've been out for two hours, caught three little crocs and nearly been chewed twice each. It's not worth it.'

'Roger,' I agreed. 'But I want to go give Tripod some love before we head home. I've got a chook for him.'

He rolled his eyes. 'You're obsessed with that animal, Matty. The way you talk about him, it's like he's a fluffy puppy.'

It was true, there was something about Tripod. I felt like he knew who I was and vice versa. He was my mate.

We drove over to his pen but it was empty. We noticed that his fence had been knocked down during the recent renovations, so we drove around the entire park looking for him for an hour but couldn't find him.

'He's gone walkabout in the open area,' I said to Jimmy.

But he wanted out. 'Mate, I don't think we're going to find him tonight. It's 1 a.m., let's come back another time.'

So we left.

Even though I was fed up with catching the small crocs I kept at it until the end of breeding season, using it as a way to scour the park, searching for Tripod. The whole park holds more than 1000 breeding crocodiles, so trying to locate one particular croc in a cast of a thousands was a challenge. I had no luck for 12 weeks. By that point, I was sure he was gone, and had been beaten in a battle.

The scenery at night-time and the movements of crocs was unbelievable, so I took my camera out on one of the last nights of breeding season. I headed out to a part of the farm where a large pond is canopied by trees. It's called Jurassic Park, and is home to about 30 enormous males. It was a full moon with a clear sky – the lighting was insane.

I brought my mate Jai along with me. I worded him up.

'There's a lot of big fellas in the one waterhole, so this could get interesting,' I told him. 'Just have your wits about you.'

'When isn't it interesting with you, Matt?' Jai replied.

The moment I hopped out of the ute a small croc showed interest and chased me around a little woodpile. Jai had to run out in her periphery and entice her over his way with a stick for her to chew on.

'Far out, there's always one cranky one,' I remarked.

I shone my torch across the pond and, standing in front of me, about 10 metres away, was Tripod.

'Hey, my man!' I called out. God, it made me happy to see him.

He started slugging his way towards me and, at the same time, a beautiful spectacle unfolded right in front of my eyes. At least 20 smaller crocodiles, from different spots around the pond's edge, speared through the air and into the water at the exact same time. It was like synchronised diving. I kicked myself for missing the shot, but I had a pig leg in my hand and a croc coming at me.

'That was the sickest thing I've ever seen!' Jai called out.

'I'm with you there,' I agreed. Then I remembered Tripod, who was still making his way towards me. 'Come on, hey! Come onnnn. Come on. Hey, come onnnn!' I continued, echoing out my usual call while I slapped a pig leg on the ground, causing vibrations and bringing him closer.

Tripod would have recognised the sound of my ute's

engine and associated it with a feed. He stopped a few feet away from me and waited patiently. The algae in the water had given him a slimy green coat, which shone fluorescent in the moonlight. He looked supernatural. I walked behind him, giving him a good rub and taking some pictures of his striking colour. He gulped down his pig leg and then slowly returned to the water, heading back out into its depths.

Without warning, he launched with full gusto at a 14-foot croc to his right, engulfing it in his jaws and thrashing it around like it was a rag doll. The other croc tried to wriggle away, but Tripod crunched and snapped down on him some more before flinging him through the air and back onto the bank, before continuing into the water. The mangled croc lay there on the shore, lifeless.

I was shocked. I've never forgotten that moment because I witnessed this usually docile, slow and lazy crocodile turn into a killing machine in an instant. No matter how laid-back Tripod seems to me I am never ever complacent with him, because even though he knows me he'd still eat me if ever given the chance.

I knew that same fate could very easily happen to Tripod given his disability and I didn't want him to end up that way, so I asked the owner of the croc farm if I could get a permit from Parks and Wildlife and keep him as a pet at my place.

'You can have him, if you find him and work out how to move him,' the owner said to me.

I got moving on the offer before he changed his mind and thought it was fitting to call Nick Robinson and get him involved in the relocation, given the history. Nick, Willow and I returned the next morning with a tilt tray, crane, equipment and a strategy. Enticed with a chook, Tripod slunk out of the waterhole and straight towards me. He stopped at my feet and even opened his jaws, making it so easy to slip a rope over his snout. I couldn't believe it. It was plain sailing and I had him just like that. Willow jumped in behind me and we began to pull him towards the back of the tilt tray.

And that was when Tripod decided to flip out. He flung around, kicking us both on our arses. We immediately scrambled up but we couldn't regain control of him. He took off and we had no choice but to start skiing on the end of the rope behind him, through the mud towards the water, where a heap of other crocs would have happily met our arrival. Nick came running in to help. He grabbed the rope and dug his heels into the mud, throwing more deadweight on the end of the rope. We finally held Tripod in one position, albeit on an obscure angle.

'Okay, you fellas, hold tight while I get some drugs in him,' Nick instructed. He darted around to Tripod's tail and jabbed him with the dose. Finally, after 20 minutes of awkwardly wedging ourselves into the ground to hold him still, he fell asleep. We secured him safely and used the crane to lift him onto the mattress on the back of the tilt-tray truck.

It was impressive watching the crane lift a 17-foot, one-tonne animal into the air and onto a queen-size mattress. We got it done with ease, and Tripod stayed calm (and asleep) the entire time. I had a 30-tonne digger at home, so I got a few of my mates to hook in and cut out a big hole in less than 48 hours. We filled it with water, added a high, sturdy fence, and dropped Tripod into his new home at the back of my property.

The most common question I get asked by people, by media in particular, is 'How old is Tripod?' The truth is, I don't really know. It's always been a bit of a guesstimate, but I usually say he's between 70 and 80 years old, mainly because of his large size and the fact that crocodiles don't ever stop growing over their lifetimes so, in theory, the bigger the croc is the older it should be. However, this notion is also a little flawed because it doesn't take into account genetics, diet and whether the croc has lived in captivity or not – all factors that would affect the growth rate of a croc. Additionally, determining the age of crocodiles is tricky because they live for such a long time and, quite simply, reliable age records are hard to come by.

I feel confident saying that Tripod is between 70 and 80 years old because the average age of a saltwater crocodile is 70 years, and some have been said to live up to 110, so 70 to 80 seems like a realistic, even conservative, age range to me. Another thing that not a lot of people know about crocs is they show almost zero signs of aging. In other words, a 10-year-old crocodile matches a 100-year-old one in terms of their physical capabilities. This biological immortality is referred to as negligible senescence, and very few animals have it. It's pretty cool to think that crocs never age or deteriorate, and that their only real chance of dying is via disease, misfortune or a predator. It's no wonder they've been around for 200 million years.

Tripod has been happily homed at my place for nearly 10 years now, and in that time has become a social media sensation. Videos and pictures of Tripod reach millions of people around the world who are in awe of his dinosaur-like presence.

I've never had a close call with Tripod in my daily interactions with him, but I do remember one incident that nearly cost me a limb. I give Tripod's pen a good clean-out a couple of times a year. On this particular occasion I'd pumped him in some fresh water, cleared out loose debris and was whipper-snippering the long grass in his pen. I climbed a tree on my way over to a patch of grass on the other side and cut a couple of its branches down in the process to clean things up. As I swung myself around the tree with my left hand, ready to launch in the air and jump off around the other side, Tripod's massive jaws slammed down at my feet.

'Holy shit!'

I shifted my foot up the next flimsy tree branch, with the whipper snipper still turned on in my right hand. Tripod snapped again, going for the whipper snipper. I had no one around to deter him and this tree, which was more like a scrub bush, was no place to retreat for safety. I fidgeted and fumbled with the snipper, eventually finding the 'off' button at the same time as Tripod manoeuvred himself up at me again.

In the same motion, I had to jump from my position in the tree to the ground and use the whipper snipper as my defence stick, like I do on crocodile nests, prodding and poking him back into the water. He had a couple more cracks, but once he realised there was nothing different to see he retreated.

I can't believe I was so silly not to think that the sound of the motor would draw him out of the water. Whether it's a boat engine, a car idling or a lawnmower running, crocs are always drawn to those mechanical sounds. I only half-tidied his pen that time and am pretty wary with any sounds around him these days.

I love the big fella and I will be very interested to see how long he hangs around for. He's pretty unlikely to catch a disease, he's not going to get eaten by anything and he's fed more than enough food, so maybe Tripod will stand the test of time and continue to grow and outlive all of us!

8

Hiccups and headaches

Anyone who knows me knows that I am the king of grand ideas and love nothing more than showing people a good time. A lot of my business decisions have favoured making people happy over making lots of money, which any good businessman will know is the first way to go arse-up pretty quick. Instead of crunching numbers and looking at the commercial viability of something, I tend to imagine the coolest, most unique and adventurous business idea and work back from there, which, again, is good for your soul but not your back pocket. To add to this combination, I also have a habit of biting off more than I can chew and my expectations of what I can achieve are often far greater than what eventuates. And there is no better example of where these personality traits of mine come into play than my first large-scale tourism endeavour, Outback Floatplane Adventures.

I love life in the Territory, whether it's flying my chopper, catching crocs, fishing or exploring the outback. I truly believe that life doesn't get much better and I've always had a desire to share it with people. Over the years I've dreamt up a range of weird and wonderful ideas, but I kept coming back to an adventure with crocs, choppers, airboats, fishing and four-wheel driving. But I didn't know where I would do it, I didn't have access to any land, I didn't have a plane to reach remote locations, and I had no cash to invest in it, so my dream stayed a dream for a long time.

In 2011, I got a gig flying some high-end lads on a corporate trip around the Kimberley, where we visited what David Attenborough refers to as one of the modern natural wonders of the world, the Horizontal Falls. I met a bloke called Troy Thomas, who'd started a small tourism operation out there off the back of a fishing charter company. He grew it over the years to eventually comprise an all-inclusive trip with a seaplane, jetboats, choppers and a pontoon structure with overnight accommodation. The tour actually went on to be named the number-one adventure tour in Australia. The lads and I booked one of Troy's overnight tours while we were in the area, and Troy and I hit it off straight away. I told him about my idea for a tourism operation in the Territory, and we agreed then and there that we'd do something. Again, going into business with someone I'd shared beers with over a couple of days was another brash decision on my behalf, but it felt right so I went with it.

We became business partners and Outback Floatplane Adventures was born. With it came a testing but triumphant journey that was full of hiccups, headaches, hard work and an absolute labour of love to bring a new high-quality tourism experience to the Northern Territory.

Troy and I agreed that the tour would involve a floatplane flight from Darwin, which would land at a remote water location and dock on a pontoon set-up. From there, we would take guests for a river cruise, followed by a rainforest tour in an airboat, a scenic flight in a helicopter, and finishing with a little off-road Polaris quad-bike adventure. It took us 10 months from the time Troy and I met until our first day of operation. I already owned a chopper, Troy was sending his 12-metre cruise vessel, *Cyclone Creek*, from Broome, Troy's dad, Reece, a veteran pilot, helped us secure a floatplane and the Polaris and pontoons were easy enough to organise. The one thing that Troy and I both didn't know much about at the time was airboats, so I left the sourcing and purchasing with Troy, who then passed the job onto a middleman by the name of Brendan Smith, an 'airboat specialist'. Well, what a mistake that was.

Troy looped me in on a quick three-way phone call with Brendan to go over the plan for obtaining the airboats, and the pricing.

'Righto, lads,' Brendan said. 'Diamondback Airboats in Orlando, Florida, is the best in the business, so we'll get everything done in the States. Instead of using their petrol V8 engines, let's put a Duramax Diesel fuel-injector engine in. It will have way more grunt.'

I followed the conversation along with the odd 'okay' and 'Sounds good' but didn't have much to add. This guy was the specialist, so I figured I'd leave it to him.

'And pricing?' Troy asked.

'You'll be looking at 150,000 Australian dollars and a 14-seat airboat delivered to your doorstep in Darwin. I've got it all covered so, if you're happy with the price, leave it with me and I'll get it to you in three months.'

'Roger, sounds good,' I said, and we both agreed to go ahead, paying our deposit directly to Brendan.

Every now and then, a group email came through from Diamondback Airboats with picture updates of the boat. A couple of times the team in Orlando raised their concerns about the use of a different engine, but Brendan always wrote back to them, insisting it would be fine. After construction of the boat was underway, Brendan told us he needed to fly to Orlando to ensure that the airboat met all of our survey requirements with the correct flotation, safety rails and equipment, so we paid for his flights, accommodation and associated costs.

The requests continued to roll in after his return. Brendan asked for an additional $5000 for more engine parts, $15,000 for freighting, and other dribs and drabs for cash reimbursements. The airboat was starting to cost us in excess of $170,000, and I smelt something fishy. Troy knew Brendan, but I was yet to meet him in person and I didn't have a good feeling about him. When the time came for the final product to be delivered, we were told that the airboat's arrival into Brisbane had been delayed by two weeks, which meant it would be another four weeks until it made it to Darwin. I called Brendan to see what was going on.

'Can you shed some light on what's happening, Brendan?'

'Oh, hey, Matt, yeah it's just one of those things, mate. When you're transporting something from country to country, timings can change. Don't stress, I'm going to base myself here in Brisbane until the boat arrives, at no charge to you guys, to make sure I see it to Darwin without a glitch.'

'Oh, so you're in Brisbane already?' I asked.

'Yeah, mate, yeah, I am,' he replied.

Things just seemed off with him. I hung up the phone and did some sniffing around over the next week or so. Ten days later I saw a picture on Facebook of Brendan at the Sanctuary Cove Boat Show on the Gold Coast – and he was there with our airboat promoting it!

I called Troy, overwhelmed with rage. 'You've got to be shitting me!' I shouted. 'That broker is a bloody shark! Our boat is here, and he's got it on the Gold Coast. He's taken it down to the boat show and is telling people it's his boat and that he can build airboats like this in Australia!'

'Ya kidding!' Troy replied. 'What a con artist. I'll get onto him now and get him AND the boat up to Darwin to have some words.'

I was flat out organising all of the other moving parts of our new business, and the last thing I needed was this headache.

Troy called me to say he'd spoken with Brendan. 'He apologised for taking it and not keeping us in the loop. Apparently he didn't think it would be an issue.'

'I don't know what planet he lives on to think that's okay!' I snapped back.

'Yeah,' Troy agreed. 'But there's one more thing. The flea doesn't even have transport organised to Darwin like he promised.'

I couldn't even respond to this, so he continued. 'And that's not the worst of it: he's just left our airboat in the convention centre car park in Brisbane, so I've just had to organise its collection and transport.'

I was absolutely dumbfounded that someone could do this sort of thing.

'I didn't reveal to Brendan how livid we are because I don't want to scare him off coming to Darwin,' Troy said.

'Good! I at least want the opportunity to have it out with him!' I replied.

The airboat arrived in Darwin two weeks later. Even though it had cost us an arm and a leg we were excited to finally see it in the flesh, and we took it straight out to Manton Dam to test it. We pulled the cover off.

'Far out, Troy,' I remarked. 'Look at the state of this thing. This Brendan fella has burnt us in the arse something fierce.' There was grease, sand, scuff marks and even chewing gum all over the floor. He must have had people walking on it at the show.

The flooring was made of non-greasy sea deck, which usually looks great but not when someone has trodden all over it with shit on their feet. Gee, I was wild. In a way, it was my own fault for not having my finger on the pulse, but setting everything else up with the business had me preoccupied. I had trusted that Troy had the right contacts, but he was just as busy as I was and didn't have time to oversee things.

I always give people the benefit of the doubt and presume they are as honest and fair, but sadly I continued to be proven wrong more times than I did right. My mate Macca, who lives locally in Darwin and owns an airboat himself, came out to test drive the airboat with us and give us his thoughts. We finally got the airboat in the water and, five minutes in, it stopped with error messages showing up.

'Yeah, guys, this engine is shithouse,' Macca told us. 'The boat is perfect, but this engine isn't made for this sort of thing. It's no good.'

Again, I just had nothing to say and Macca continued with his thoughts.

'Sure, a Duramax engine is the duck's nuts if you're putting it into a Dodge Ram but NOT an airboat. This thing is triple the weight of a normal airboat engine, and the boat's going to lag because of it.'

At this point, nothing he said surprised me. I was sitting there in silence, imagining all the different ways I could give Brendan the karma he deserved.

Troy tried to be a little more positive. 'Sure, it's got a lot of torque, but the immediate power isn't quite there.'

'Mate, it's the power you need the most. That's what gets an airboat up on land and gives it the lift it needs. Imagine if this had 14 passengers on it,' Macca added.

'Yeah, it would be impossible to manoeuvre,' I agreed.

The key to an airboat's power is instant velocity and this

dumb-arse Brendan had not only asked to make the width of the boat thinner, which took away the water displacement on the hull, but then fitted a heavy engine without the pick-up power. And this engine had cost double the price of a normal Chevy V8 engine, which is absolutely perfect for airboat use. It was all a mess.

I called Diamondback in Florida, which I should have done a lot earlier, and started asking questions. What I heard from them just added to my disappointment.

Diamondback (which, for the record, is an awesome airboat company) had never dealt with Brendan before this ordeal. And Brendan had tried to take the airboat out of the workshop while he was in Orlando before he finished paying for it, plus he actually ripped Diamondback off, putting a ten-thousand-dollar payment on a bogus credit card. Unfortunately, after trying my damnedest to help Diamondback recover this money we had no luck and were unable to ever get the payment.

Everything was completely embarrassing. We had really been taken for a run and the worst part was that the conning didn't stop there. I clarified with Diamondback which foam they put in the airboat and it was nothing close to what we needed to meet our survey requirements. Brendan had instructed Diamondback to put polyester foam underneath the hull, which is like what you would have on a normal foam cooler box. This sort of foam isn't fire- or fuel-resistant, so if we were to get fuel on it, the foam would disintegrate and turn into a napalm gel, transforming the boat into a floating bomb and if that didn't cause the boat to blow up it would certainly sink. We had this new one hundred and seventy-thousand-dollar boat that wasn't even water-worthy.

So there I was the next day, in my shed with my beautiful new airboat, pulling out the seats, flooring and sea deck, and cutting through everything with a hot knife. I was crawling into crevices only a cat could reach, sucking in fumes and coughing my guts up. It ended up taking me two whole days to pull out the foam, replace it and refabricate the boat while I uttered every single swearword known to mankind. I was putting my life savings into this business and some weasel was trying to ruin me. It was the worst feeling. I was heartbroken. And the foam was the final straw.

I called Brendan, trying to remain as calm as possible, not letting on how upset I was. 'Hey mate, just checking to see if you're still planning on coming up next week and if you need me to book you accommodation?' I asked when he answered the phone.

'Hey, Matt, yeah that would be great. Looking forward to seeing the boat in the water!' he said, all excited.

'Yep, and I'm looking forward to seeing you too, mate,' I said, through gritted teeth.

I put the airboat to the back of my mind and focused on the rest of the set-up. I figured I'd wait for Brendan to reach Darwin before making any more major decisions, because I planned on getting him to foot the bill for a new engine at the very least. We only had eight weeks left until the tour launched and I had far more important things to work out, like which location we were going to run out of.

Because I collected crocodile eggs during the wet season, I knew every waterhole, nook and cranny around the Territory. I'd been flying over the landscape for the past 15 years and had earmarked two places that I thought would be able to handle our tour and that were under 30 minutes flying time from Darwin. One was called Bull Coin and the other was Sweets Lagoon. I locked in a time to fly out there with Reece and Troy for a reconnaissance-type mission. Reece flew us out in a little Cessna 182, which we attached floats to so we could land on water.

We tested the first spot at Bull Coin. Landing on a big waterhole, we all hopped out and immediately felt pretty underwhelmed by our surroundings. Don't get me wrong, it's beautiful country but it was too open and just wasn't right for what we were after. We returned to Darwin and switched from the Cessna to my chopper so I could take Reece and Troy for a fly to the second spot, Sweets Lagoon. Willow came along for the ride too.

I'd shown the guys the area before and Reece, who had been flying for many years, didn't think we could land a floatplane on the water strip because he felt it was too small, but I was sure we could and took everyone for a closer look. I flew down through the trees and along the water strip to give Reece a better perspective. I pointed out where the floatplane would land and where the pontoon set-up would go.

'You're right, mate, this won't be a problem at all. We'll just have to clear out the thick grass, floating mat and logs so the plane floats don't hit the crap on landing,' Reece said.

We were stoked with the area. The main lagoon was a prehistoric paradise abundant with wildlife, and we knew it would blow the public away. We wanted to operate there but had no idea who owned the land or how to access it from the main road.

After flying around some more, I spotted a few dirt roads, a mango farm and a little shack in an overgrown area. I landed at the shack. It was totally rundown and clearly unoccupied. There was tall gammon grass growing right to the top of the roof and old scrap metal lying around the place. It looked like a junkyard.

I pushed the front door open with my foot and walked into Noah's Ark. There was a pig wallow in one corner with a couple of feral boars moving about, a couple of bandicoots scurried around, and a possum ran along the ceiling beam.

'Ahh!' Willow jumped aside to make way for a wallaby that came bounding out of the kitchen. It hopped past us and out the door. We all laughed at where we were and what was going on. The front door of the shack opened up to a large concrete breezeway, which was screened at either end, and there was a bathroom, kitchen and toilet on one side and three rooms with air-conditioning units on the other (whether they worked or not was another story!). There was worn-out furniture around the place and most of the flyscreens were torn apart. The floor was covered in bat shit and other faeces from the menagerie of animals living in there. I did a quick poke around the kitchen, which had all the basics. I opened a gas oven and out slithered a decent-sized brown snake. 'Jesus! It's been yonks since anyone's been in here!' I tailed the animal, walked outside and let it go in the bushes.

We walked along a narrow road nearby overgrown with pandan plants, shrubs and small trees. It would need a lot of slashing and grading for us to be able to get from the shack down the two-kilometre dirt road to the lagoon. We finished off the rest of our recce and flew home. There was no question, we all had our hearts set on Sweets Lagoon and the shack.

I discovered that the lagoon was on crown land, so we could operate there but I still needed to work out who owned what around the water and the shack: was it private property or Indigenous land? The next day I flew back there and started conversations with Paul Venturin from Finniss River Station. His fence line ran into the lagoon on one side, so I got permission to access the lagoon from his land to begin with, just to get the equipment in. He gave me the details of David, a Vietnamese man who owned the land directly connected to the lagoon as well as the shack. I planned on reaching out to him at some point too.

A week later, we trucked *Cyclone Creek* to Sweets Lagoon along with another truck to cart two front-end loaders equipped with forklifts and buckets. The seven-kilometre dirt road from Cox Peninsula Road to the station boundary was full of divots, culverts and holes, and recent rain meant that it was wet and muddy. The truck got stuck a couple of times and the lads had to drive the loaders off the second truck to pull the main truck out.

Eventually we reached the boundary and cut the fence. Taking the boat down through the paddock was easy going until we reached a patch of large cathedral termite mounds, which we had to zig zag through until we finally got to the only spot that would allow us to get close enough to the river to slide the boat in. We flattened a pad with the loaders and created it on a bit of an angle to help edge the boat into the water. There was a large five-foot-round solid melaleuca paperback tree on the other side of the bank. I figured I could hook a block and tackle onto the tree and create a big pulley system with the front-end loaders and the boat. That way, when the loaders went back, the boat would slide forward into the water.

I thought the job would be a headache, but it ended up working really well.

'This is the easiest thing we've had to do out of everything!' I said to Troy and the crew. The boat was in and it was time for the trickier part – getting it through a clogged-up channel about three metres wide. It was just after the wet season, so there had been constant rain with trees falling down all over the shop. This particular part of the river was like a beaver dam – it was totally clogged up with logs, floating mat and debris. We had to clear it all out to fit the boat through. The work needed to be done anyway, because a beaver dam locks a river up and stops the flow of water, which is bad for the environment. Healthy waterways need to flow so that the fish and aqua life can continually move around.

Macca had his airboat out with us. My mate Steve and I jumped on the front with Mac and he steered the way through the debris, breaking everything up like a food processor. Every so often Mac had to stop the airboat so I could cut up some of the bigger logs lying in the water. Towards the end of the channel, we came across an entire trunk laying right in our path. Stepping out carefully, I started cutting from the opposite end to where the trunk was still half-wedged into the ground. I cut slowly and carefully until I was suddenly taken by surprise: I felt the trunk give way underneath me.

Plunging into the water with the chainsaw blaring I thought I was cactus. The chainsaw fell on top of my right arm as I hit the water, nipping me with a painful sting. I resurfaced holding the chainsaw away from me with my good arm. Blood was pouring out, turning the water red. Macca leant down and grabbed the chainsaw from me, passed it to Steve and pulled me up.

'Heck, Matty, give me a look at ya!' Mac said, worry spread across his face.

I was dreading seeing the damage. 'I don't know, Mac, but it bloody hurts. Let's make sure I'm all connected still,' I said, jokingly. I was in pain but trying to make light of the situation.

Much to my amazement, after cleaning it up I was relieved to see a large surface-cut – nothing too serious. I got lucky and was even luckier that someone was there to help me back onto the boat, because bleeding out in croc-infested waters is a death sentence.

There was a really dense bit of mat right at the end of the channel before the lagoon opened up and we just couldn't break it with the airboat, we had to go back and forth over it, throwing anchors and big poles trying to separate it. After two hours, we had broken the mat up as much as possible and lifted the motors on *Cyclone Creek*, so it could glide over without damage. We finally broke onto the open lagoon, and everyone boarded the big boat and opened the beers to celebrate. We put some tunes on and took her up the river for a cruise before dropping the anchor and calling it a day.

Early the next morning I flew the chopper back to the lagoon to do some reconnaissance for the pontoon placement. I landed on the helipad on top of *Cyclone Creek* and walked down the stairs to see a letter sitting on the kitchen bench with a rock on it.

Please call to discuss plans. I'm at the mango farm all day. David.

I booted straight over in the chopper and met up with David, the owner of the land next to the lagoon, and the shack. I started explaining what I wanted to do, but he didn't seem keen on the idea.

'No tourism here, sorry. It's too dangerous, too many bad people!' he said.

'What do you mean?' I asked.

'People come and steal off me,' he told me. 'The pig hunters, they come and they steal diesel, shoot the pigs and cut my fences.'

He was a lovely guy who'd had a bad run and I felt sorry for him. He told me that someone had even tried to steal his forklift recently but ran out of petrol at the front gate.

'Look,' I said. 'I would love to rent your shack off you and do it up. We would use it and the road down to the lagoon. I'll put up proper security, help grade your roads and make the place look brand new again and I promise there won't be any more trouble on the property.'

David was hesitant, for obvious reasons. He didn't know me, I didn't know him, but Paul from Finniss River Station had put in a good word and so David agreed to give me a go. We worked out a land-use agreement for the first 12 months. The shack had a little generator and a bore, so we had power and water, which is all that matters in the bush.

At this point I had secured the lagoon, the shack and access to the shared road. I was on a roll, and it was time for Brendan's arrival into Darwin.

My mate Macca is a big, burly bloke with an intimidating presence, so I asked him to pick Brendan up from the airport and bring him straight to the shack. Mac knew about Brendan's dodgy business and was furious about the whole thing.

'Don't worry, Matty,' he assured me. 'I'll sort this Brendan guy out and make sure we get your airboat going.' And then off he went.

Troy and I were pressure-cleaning the shack when Macca's car pulled up. Out hopped Brendan with a beer-carton box wrapped around his hips. He shuffled towards the shack door.

'Is there a shower in there?' he asked, on the way through.

'Huh?' I replied.

But Brendan didn't stop to say anything else, he just kept heading for the bathroom.

'What happened, Mac?' Troy asked.

'I just gave him the shake-up he deserved and told him to sort his mess out before things turn ugly. I think the pressure was too much for the poor guy and he soiled himself. He came back to the car with his pants off, smelling like shit, so I had to sort him out with the box,' Mac said.

'He what?' Troy asked.

'His pants. He pooed them,' Macca said, in a matter-of-fact way.

I'd never seen anything like it, but I didn't ask Mac any more questions. I figured he'd laid down the law and he'd got the message through. I chucked a pair of old shorts at the door for Brendan because I didn't particularly want him wandering around naked. He appeared a little while later, speechless, sitting down at the trestle table outside. I couldn't stand to look at him.

'Troy, I actually can't even look at the bloke. I thought I could face him, but the sight of him just makes me sick. Macca's told him he needs to cover our new airboat engine, so that's it from me. I'm not going to waste my breath,' I said.

'I'll sort him out, then,' Troy said, speaking like Brendan wasn't even around. He turned to Brendan. 'Come on, ya flea. I'll take you back to Darwin. You're not welcome here.'

Brendan stood up and walked away with his head down, not saying a word. That was the last I ever saw of the guy. We engaged lawyers to get our money back, but it turned out he had nothing. His wife had taken him to the cleaners and he'd ripped off a heap of other people, so we were just one of the many. We would have spent more in legal fees trying to fight him, but I truly believe that every dog has their day. We had to foot the bill for the new engine from America, which cost another twenty-five thousand US dollars plus the money for shipping, air freight and installation. After the mess-around from Brendan, we worked out that the airboat cost us a quarter of a million Australian dollars. A big blow to a new business, but we kept pushing on.

We finally had the new engine, and got the airboat onto the lagoon. The machine was perfect, but Troy's and my driving was far from it. We weren't at all savvy to start with. On Troy's first expedition he sideswiped a tree, denting the cage, and on my first adventure I took a corner a little too hard and ended up high and dry.

At least Troy made it home after his incident, whereas I ended up in the middle of the rainforest, stranded. In the process of banking myself I cleaned up a tree, jerking the boat, creating an almighty bang as the props went ballistic and the engine screamed until it came to a standstill. I had no mobile, no sat phone and no radio. I knew Steve was on *Cyclone Creek* with the chopper because I could hear music playing in the distance. I was in prime croc territory, so I grabbed a stick, legged it to an elevated point and started yelling. I yelled and yelled and yelled for a good 10 minutes and eventually the music stopped. I yelled again and then again. And all of a sudden I heard the chopper start.

'Yes, he's heard me!'

I watched Steve fly around, looking in all the wrong places. He was four days into having his chopper licence and the poor guy was on a search and rescue mission AND I was about to signal him instructions for a very tricky landing to pick me up.

He eventually spotted me and I had him come in and land in this extremely tight area, light on his skids so I could jump in the machine and get out of there. He was a little slow, but he did it with precision and I was very impressed.

Then it was time to tow the airboat out, fix it up AGAIN and get it back on the water, which took another couple of days. Believe it or not, things with the airboat improved after that and it ran glitch-free for most of our first tour season.

We bought one of our pontoons second-hand and Troy arranged for another two to be built. Once we got them to the shack, I had to airlift them in an R66 helicopter. I started with the biggest of the three, using a ratchet strap to sling the pontoon under the chopper. It was one I used to tie things down on the back of my trailer. It wasn't the best choice, but it was doing the job fine until a gust of wind came through.

The strap blew underneath the main hook, twisted and released itself and began floating down. All I could do was sit there and watch as a ten-thousand-dollar pontoon flew through the air.

'Oh noooo, oh noooo. Please land on the floating mat, please land on the floating mat,' I said as it flipped and floated down further and further below. One section landed on the mat and the other part hit hard into the water, shattering and bending on impact. I landed to assess the situation. It was totally unsalvageable.

I used the airboat to tow it back to the landing. No one said a word. They all would have known exactly what I was feeling and how annoyed I would have been at myself. I secured the other pontoons with double the amount of straps and got them out safely.

I had to fix the pontoons to the bottom of the lagoon. Steve was on the lookout for crocs while I swam down to fix the mooring lines to the cleats. It was challenging enough fiddling with the pontoons and moorings, let alone the fact I was in the heart of croc country. It was bloody scary swimming below the surface because I knew there were 16-foot man-eaters in the area, and I was fully aware of the love that crocs have for engines, after many incidents with my pet Tripod and his interest in metallic grinding sounds!

After an hour of being on edge, I eventually got the pontoons fixed with all limbs intact. We were a week out from launching by this point and Steve, Mac and I finished the day off on one of the airboat rainforest tracks. We were waist-deep in crystal-clear water, cutting the last of the floating branches. I wasn't too concerned about getting chomped on because I could see our surrounds so clearly. I got caught up in the job at hand and dropped my guard. In the corner of my eye I saw this shadow underneath the water coming towards us.

'Holy hell, that looks like a crocodile. Shit, it is! Croc, croc, croc, get out!' I yelled. Ditching everything in our hands we scooted up onto the airboat and out popped this croc, right where we were. She was only eight foot and a skinny little animal.

'Well, aren't you a sweet thing?' Mac said.

'She's sweet when we're out of the water, not so much when we're in it,' I said.

'All right, sweet thing, see ya next time!'

We named the croc Sweet Thing and she became one of the resident crocs at Sweets Lagoon, always popping her head up in the same place to say g'day to guests on tour.

Then it was time to add the final piece of the Outback Floatplanes puzzle, the Polaris. It was too heavy to swing underneath the chopper, so we pulled out the seats on Macca's airboat and putted the new 800-kilogram buggy across the lagoon at a snail's pace.

'Mac, please, take it slow. I can't afford to have this buggy end up at the bottom of the lagoon. We've had enough disasters for now.'

'Yeah mate, yeah mate, it will be fine,' Mac said, without a care in the world. 'I'll take it steady, don't worry.'

Macca's 'steady' is like a bull at a gate at the best of times, but he did us proud and got the buggy safely to the other side of the lagoon. I couldn't believe it. After 10 months of going harder than I ever had before, we had everything ready. I had no cash left to my name, was completely sleep-deprived and had lost a ton of weight from all the stress, but had a sense of pride like never before. I had a dream, took a risk (actually, I took a number of risks), and I made it happen. A lot of people told me I was nuts and I know a lot of people thought that Troy and I couldn't do it, but we did.

Our first tour ran in 2012 with seven guests who absolutely loved it, and things grew from there. We ran tours on top of tours, and the bookings continued to roll in with five-star reviews. In the first six months we had become the number-one tour in Darwin on TripAdvisor and were running three tours a day, seven days a week. It was the best thing I had ever achieved, and it was great for the Territory.

In early 2018, I sold my share of Outback Floatplane Adventures to Troy so I could focus on other business opportunities and filming for *Outback Wrangler*. It was very hard to part with the business because of everything I put into it, but it still runs today and I'm proud of the small legacy I left behind.

9
Island adventure

The Osborne Islands are found on the eastern side of the Admiralty Gulf in Kimberley country, WA. They are both beautiful and forbidding with large cliffy islands surrounded by rocks, smaller isles and impressive waterfalls. This remote part of the world is best known for its surface pearl farms owned and operated by Australian South Sea pearling company Paspaley. A mothership, barges, Mallard seaplanes, farm workers and crew support the operations.

But Osborne's striking turquoise waters aren't just filled with white gems, they're also home to a high population of sharks and saltwater crocodiles. Divers navigate the ocean's perils with strategies in place to keep them out of the jaws of these hungry predators. But, back in 2014, one particular croc started causing headaches. No matter where the divers went, this curious croc was there, and one day the big fella got too close for comfort. A bloke was sitting on the edge of one of the barges and got a rude shock when the croc launched up and missed him by an inch. They decided that something had to be done.

Paspaley didn't feel right about getting a permit to kill the croc, so they called me up to see if I'd be interested in relocating it. I'd never faced a challenge like it – catching a saltwater crocodile in open ocean was no easy feat. I had no idea at the time how the hell I'd manage the job, but I wasn't going to pass up this unique opportunity. And besides, the job had all the right ingredients for my favourite thing in life: adventure.

'I'm all over it!' I said down the phone to the Paspaley operations manager. 'Leave it with me and I'll get back to you with a plan. Just one thing, though: do you think I'll be able to film it for the show?'

'I don't see why not,' the Paspaley bloke replied.

With a shit-heaped grin on my face, I hung up the phone and got planning.

•

Paspaley was going to supply me with all the equipment and a dedicated Mallard seaplane to relocate the crocodile to the mainland. I also spoke to the Indigenous traditional landowners to let them know what was happening, contacted the Parks and Wildlife Commission of the Northern Territory, and asked Willow and Jono to give me a hand with the logistics of it all.

I came across my first hurdle during my meeting with NT Parks and Wildlife.

'Where are you going to put the croc once you catch it, Matty?' the head ranger, Tommy Nichols, asked me. 'The croc is in WA waters, not the Territory, so I don't like your chances of getting it back to a park here.'

'Shit,' I replied. 'I didn't think of that.'

I got on the blower to WA Parks and Wildlife, who confirmed what Tommy had said. So, my next port of call was the Malcolm Douglas Crocodile Park. Malcolm, who was famous for his 1968 Australian doco series *Across the Top*, opened a popular croc park near Broome's Cable Beach in 1983. After his sudden death in 2010 all of the crocs moved to the current park with better facilities, which his wife, Valerie, continues to run.

The new park is located about 15 minutes outside of Broome, and was going to be the closest and most practical option for the Osborne Islands croc. Valerie didn't want a bar of me or the croc, but unfortunately for her she was obliged to take it because WA Parks and Wildlife requested we keep it in WA and send it to her park, which was the only suitable place with capacity at the time.

'I don't want to be a part of your bloody filming spectacle. I've got no time for you or this,' she told me when I called her to make arrangements.

'Sorry we're not seeing eye to eye here, Valerie, but I look forward to seeing you in a couple of months when we drop the croc off. It will be great to meet you,' I said, trying the 'kill them with kindness' technique.

'Whatever, you idiot,' she replied, and hung up abruptly.

It was a shame she was so hostile. I had the croc's best interests at heart but it seemed like she didn't give a shit about it. Nevertheless, she signed the relocation agreement, so I had that box ticked.

It was the height of the wet season in 2016 and Jono and I were in the thick of collecting croc eggs, so Willow got the guernsey to do the reconnaissance. I sent him over in the Mallard seaplane with about 500 kilos of frozen pig legs stored in eskies to start baiting traps on floats. He was also going to set motion-sensor cameras along the main creek and around the outskirts of the biggest waterhole.

Willow lost a few cameras to big tides, but he managed to get footage of a couple of crocs, one of which looked like the guy we were after. More than anything, his visit gave us good intel on the crazy tides we would be dealing with, and we decided it was necessary for all three of us to go over.

We constructed four traps and got them on the Paspaley boats. We figured there would be floats there that Paspaley used for the pearling lines, so we could just attach them to the traps. It took a couple of weeks for the traps to get there, then everything was in place.

We had caught a couple of crocs at a cattle station during egg-collecting season, so Jono stayed back to organise their relocation and I booted over to the Osbornes with Willow and our cameraman, Ash. After four hours scouting the area, the reality of the job hit. The tides were so extreme – they came in and out aggressively – and looking out at the vast open ocean in front of us was overwhelming.

'Right, this is going to be one hell of a mission and we won't be able to get the job done without Jono. We need him here and we need him here now,' I said to Willow.

'Mate, the workers on the boat said there aren't any more planes coming until the next shift change in a week's time,' he replied.

I groaned. 'Ya kidding? Can we charter a light plane here? We need to get the croc now because of the way these tides are.'

Willow kept breaking the bad news to me. 'Nope, there are no airstrips. That's why they've got the Mallards, because they land on water.'

I sat there for a minute, thinking, and an idea came to me.

'Matty, you've got that sparkle in your eye like you're up to no good. What's on your mind?' Willow knows me well.

'Well, Jono has an A licence for skydiving, so let's charter a plane and get him to jump in. It'll be sick, just like *Mad Max*.'

Willow laughed, and shook his head. 'More like Mad Matt I reckon, mate.'

I don't think Willow believed me, but that arvo I called Jono, booked a plane and we made it happen.

'Check on the winds, mate, and let me know the best time to land. I'll send you the GPS spot on this little stretch of beach that I reckon will be ideal for landing,' I said to Jono over the satellite phone. I was pumped, it was all coming together. Just how I liked it.

We had our plan in place. Willow and I headed to the beach right after lunch and got the flares ready at the coordinates we'd given Jono. I had a handheld radio, so I could communicate with the pilot as they got closer. We heard the plane fly above us, and then, at 5000 feet, out popped Jono. It was game on.

He had a GoPro on him to capture the footage of the epic Kimberley scenery on the way down. He's the first and probably the last person to ever jump out of a plane over that part of the country.

Everything was going to plan but just as Jono got airborne the wind changed direction. Fuck. We had planned everything out depending on the way the wind was blowing, so when it changed unexpectedly, panic set in. I was worried, so I can't imagine what Jono was thinking when I let the flares off and he saw the way the wind was blowing.

'Shit, old son, there's not many options here,' Willow said. 'If he can't work out how to land on that narrow patch of beach it's the water or the cliffs, none of which are favourable.'

I was thinking the same thing. We were in a bit of a situation. The wind was meant to be running down along the skinny stretch of beach, so Jono could land into the wind and use the beach as a landing runway. Now that the wind was blowing perpendicular to the length of the beach it meant that he had to nail the landing on about five metres' worth of sand, otherwise he'd end up in the ocean, meeting our croc prematurely.

Jono came in closer and closer then turned his parachute in the air, coming into the wind the right way and just missing the top of the cliff. My palms were clammy with nerves. He skipped down on the rocks and over the wall to the beach. He was completely on point and came in sideways to the beach like a pro.

The whole time I was thinking, *This is nuts, we might be plucking him out of the trees here or scooping him out of the ocean.* I was second-guessing my wild idea, but it turned out okay, thank god, and he landed right next to our red flaring smoke.

'Woohoooo yewwww, Jonsy!' Willow and I ran over to him, giving high fives all around.

'Yeah, the boys!' Jono yelled back, smiling from ear to ear.

'Now let's got get this croc, hey?!' I said. We were high on life and ready to hook in to get the real job done.

Running Jonsy over everything quickly, we rebaited the traps in the areas Willow had scouted and got our first sighting on camera that night. There was the croc, coming and going from a waterhole at the top of a rocky creek that ran down into the ocean. We wanted to lure him to the waterhole rather than in the ocean's open water, so we set three traps around the big waterhole in the little channels, nooks and crannies. We got back on the Paspaley pearling mothership *Roslynne* for dinner, and the chefs cooked up fresh barramundi, which Willow and I had caught the day before. The fishing around the islands was second to none: there were one-metre-long-plus barra cruising the waters by the truckload, so anytime we had a lull during the day we were out fishing.

The next morning, we took the harpoons along to check

the traps, but I didn't like our chances of using them. It would be tough to harpoon anything in that setting because of the rocks, mangroves and barnacles. Even though we had set the traps, the waterhole itself worked as an environmental trap for us. Because saltwater crocs can live in saltwater but need fresh water to survive, they would proactively make their way up to this big open freshwater waterhole. And on a high tide, the water from the sea would rise right up to meet it, making it even easier for crocs to access. We walked over there with some of the Paspaley workers who hung around to check out the action. They told us that sometimes crocs would get stuck there high and dry when the tide went back out because, without water to lubricate the sharp rocky creek down to the ocean, it was far too rough for a croc to move along. It was our plan to keep the croc up in the waterhole with attractive bait until it got landlocked.

The other helpful part was that the waterhole would be dirty at night-time when the crazy tide hit, but then it would completely clean out in the calm of the morning, making it clear and extremely easy to see. That's how I managed our first sighting in the flesh.

'And there he is, lads!' I could see the outline of a large croc at the bottom because of the clear water but it was only partially in view, so I wasn't exactly sure if it was the right one. I took off my boots and slid into the water.

'Matty, what the hell? Are you serious?' Willow's unnerved voice called out.

'What?' I shouted back.

'You can't get in the water with the bloody croc, you're asking to get eaten! He's got the upper hand, big time.'

Jono stood there silently as Willow and I argued.

'Of course I can,' I objected. 'It's so clear, I can see everything.'

'Don't, please don't do it.'

I didn't hear the rest of Willow's pleading as I submerged myself in the chilly water to get a better look at the croc. The water was shallow in parts and deep in others, with little rocky ledges around the edge. The croc had wedged himself under one of the ledges, which is why I couldn't see his full body from out of the water. I needed to get closer to him to see if he was the croc we were after. I returned to the surface and, without even having to ask, there was Jono handing me my mask and snorkel.

'I got you, mate,' he reassured me.

Jono was standing above me at the edge of the waterhole while Willow had climbed the big formation of rocks at the back of the waterhole to get on high ground. He was pacing around like a worried parent.

'I'm going to swim right down and get a nose rope on him underwater,' I said to Jono. 'I reckon I can do it, I just need you ready to pull hard once the rope's on. He's sitting on the deepest point at the bottom, wedged into a little concave in the rock. It will be fine.'

I didn't feel nervous. Actually, I felt really focused and calm, and very connected to the croc's energy. I could tell the animal was on the run, not on the hunt.

'He's trying to hide, fellas. As long as I don't swim right up to his head I'll be okay.'

'How deep is it?' Willow called out.

'About seven feet down, I reckon! This is where all my years of free-diving on the Great Barrier will come in handy!' I yelled back.

'Go for it, Matty. I'd be in the water if it was my TV show but I'm just here to support ya, mate,' Jono said, laughing.

I laughed along with him because I knew he'd be dying to get in the water with a wild croc too, but only one of us could do it without causing too much commotion.

'Let's harpoon him and get him that way!' Willow tried convincing me otherwise.

'I'm not 100 per cent sure it's the right croc, Willow, and there's no chance with the harpoon with all these rocks and the way he's positioned.' There was no talking me out of this one. 'Willow, you keep an eye out up top and make sure there's nothing else in the water with the big guy. That's the last thing I need,' I said, and then down I went.

I chased the croc around in circles along the bottom of the waterhole but he wasn't moving out from under the ridge so I couldn't manage a clear sighting. I'd lose him momentarily every time he disturbed the ground at the bottom, creating a cloud of sand and turning the water murky. Then I'd hear a faint 'He's coming back at you!' from Willow above me. The snorkel and mask meant I could stay underwater to follow him, but I'd lose him again each time he tucked into a deep ledge. It had become a game of croc chasey. I was just glad I was the one doing the chasing. Finally, I got the croc up onto a shallow ledge situated right on a corner, which I could use as a barrier between the croc and me. I peered around the corner and saw that his tail was within reach. I gently floated to the surface to see Jono standing above.

'This is epic, Matty,' he whispered. 'You need to take the GoPro with you and get footage of this, it's nuts.'

Ash came over and I handed him my Leatherman knife. 'Gaffer-tape the GoPro to the knife so I can use it as a stand for the camera.'

I swam down and stuck the knife with the GoPro into the sand, angling the camera towards the croc. I then went back up, got the head rope and a stick, and lowered myself into the water. I poked the croc on the tail, provoking him so that he would turn towards me and, sure enough, he spun around to face me, knocking the camera flat on the ground. I can't really remember what I thought, coming face to face with a wild croc underwater, but I don't recall feeling nervous. I just did what I knew I had to do, which was getting the head rope around him as soon as possible.

He closed his jaws slowly, which was not what I wanted because I needed them open to be able to get the noose around his snout. I got the stick and jabbed him gently on the side of his jaw, which made him turn slightly to the left, and then I looped the rope around his snout. We were on.

I got out of the water as quickly as I could, tugging on the head rope in the same direction as Jono, who was pulling on the end of the rope from above water. Willow was scampering down the rocks to get on the end of the rope and help us hold the croc without all of us getting pulled into the water.

The croc was going nuts. It was thrashing around, snapping about and putting up an almighty fight. Ash was running around us, trying to get shots of the croc under water as well as shots of us pulling the croc out without slipping on the rocks or getting in our way. It was mayhem.

We found a flat surface where the water overflowed down to the creek bed. It was the perfect spot to pull the animal out. The workers called in the Paspaley operations manager to identify the croc. After a bit of manoeuvring we finally hoisted the croc up and onto dry land. And by this time the ops manager had arrived.

'Do you want the bad news or the bad news? This isn't the right croc,' the ops manager said to us. 'This one is missing part of its tail and the one we're after has its tail fully intact.'

Our excitement turned to disappointment. Jono eventually piped up. 'Oh well, that was one hell of an adventure and good practice for when we get the real guy! Let's let this fella go, then.'

It was bittersweet releasing him after the rigmarole we went through, but he wasn't a problem, so he deserved to be left alone. We walked him back along the creek bed like he was a dog on a leash, pulling him along and keeping tension on the rope. It had enough water to ease him all the way down to the ocean, where we let him go. He swam off happily.

'I think we need a beer,' I said to Willow.

'Roger that!' he replied.

We were done for the day.

•

A croc-catching mission usually takes a lot of waiting around, reassessing and changing of plans until you finally manage to get the croc you're after. This trip typified the waiting-around part, but we didn't mind. Usually in the Territory things drag on in the stinking heat, but this time we got to hang out in a Kimberley paradise with incredible swimming holes, crisp sea breezes, unbelievably insane fishing and four-course meals cooked fresh every day by the talented chefs on the *Roslynne*.

Each morning we'd check and rebait the cage traps near the waterhole then we'd go fishing, eat and have a few beers. In the early arvo we'd scout the area again, recheck the traps and hope there was a croc waiting there. We did this for a few days, but the croc was nowhere to be seen. For such an apparently inquisitive croc it didn't make sense that he'd gone to ground. We felt like we were encroaching on the workers' space too much, so we made the call to fly home.

We woke up on our last morning and shot straight down to the bottom of the creek that connected up to the waterhole. The tide was as low as we'd ever seen it. Jono, Willow and I had to walk at least a kilometre through the muddied rocks and barnacles before we reached any water. The tides had shifted the traps all over the joint. One had capsized and tipped over, another was wedged up in a tree, and one was on its side on another ledge in the waterhole. We took a closer look.

'Matty, look!' Willow yelled. 'It's a croc!'

Willow was right. A decent-sized croc was inside the third trap.

'It's got a full tail on it too!' Willow said.

'You beauty! I think we've got him.' I said, heart racing with excitement.

Jono radioed back to the *Roslynne* and let them know we had the croc. A couple of Paspaley employees turned up 30 minutes later.

'That's the one!' one of the workers said when he saw croc.

They called a crew who were back in Darwin and arranged for the next available Mallard to fly the crocodile box over for the trip to Broome. The croc was about 13 feet long, skinny, and a full-blooded little thing. We secured him in all the correct places and carried him down the creek and, with the help of the workers, onto the tender.

'The Mallard is coming in to land now. They've taken the seats out of it and put the croc box in ready to transport out of here,' one of the workers confirmed with us.

We collected our gear from the mothership and waited on the tender, ready to go. The pearly white Grumman Mallard seaplane approached in the distance. Watching the amphibious aircraft land on water is truly spectacular, and surprisingly quiet. Only a faint hissing sound can be heard as the spray of water splashes against the turbine. It is an impressive piece of machinery and the plane's white exterior really pops against the blue waters.

I administered the tranquilising drug to the croc and we got him into the box on the plane smoothly. Lots of 'thank you's were coming through from the Paspaley workers, who were relieved to see the animal moved on. An hour and a half later we were all in Broome, safely handing the croc over to Valerie. She was still less than impressed with the whole idea. But she had the space and, as much as we didn't get on, I knew she was an animal-lover and would give that Kimberley croc a good life.

10

Colossal croc

'Someone is going to get eaten soon, it's only a matter of time.'

Harold's soft voice echoed across the delayed phone line.

'Is there one croc or are there a few problems out there?' I asked him.

'Well,' Harold said, 'most of the crocs are big enough to eat any of the kids who play near the water, but there's one monster that has us all worried.'

'How big?' I asked.

'Big,' he replied with certainty.

Nobody knew the land and the crocs around Peppimenarti quite like Harold. A local traditional owner and Aboriginal Elder, Harold was born in Peppi and returned to his hometown as a young adult to raise his family. He had lived there ever since.

'Are we talking 15 foot big or 18 foot big?' I asked, trying to extrapolate more information from him.

'I reckon more like 20. He's been around since I was a kid,' he said calmly.

Nine times out of 10 I call bullshit when someone says there's a big croc, but I believed Harold. He then told me story after story about the close encounters community members had experienced with this colossal croc. And the more I heard, the more I knew that it was a job for me.

•

I planned to fly to Peppi later that week to meet Harold and scope out Tom Turner Creek, where the croc allegedly hung out. The creek ran directly alongside the small Aboriginal community of Peppimenarti, located just over 300 km southwest of Darwin. About 200 people call the town home, most of whom are local Ngan'gikurunggurr people.

Coincidentally, on the flight down to Peppi my manager, Nick Fordham, called.

'I've been chatting with *60 Minutes* and they want to fly Peter Stefanovic up to Darwin to do a segment on you and your work,' Nick told me. 'They're hoping to film soon, so we need an interesting story.'

'I think I have one,' I said. 'I'll get back to you tomorrow.'

Station owners and locals often call me to relocate crocs. I try to do as many jobs as I can and we film some of the more exciting relocations for *Outback Wrangler*. Every now and then a current-affairs show, a blogger or a print news outlet wants to do a special feature story, but it's often hard to give the media what they want because I can't just create a story or a problem croc out of thin air.

So the timing this time around was a perfect, but only if Harold was up to it.

•

Harold's warm smile greeted me as I landed the chopper.

'Let me introduce you to our people,' he said. Harold showed me around proudly, stopping me along the way to meet his family and friends. The main language spoken in Peppimenarti is Tyemirri, so Harold translated as everyone told me stories about their encounters with the infamous local croc.

A couple of women carrying newborn babies came out to see me. They started calling things out to me, sounding distressed.

Harold translated: 'They are telling you that the family dogs go down to the creek to drink, and not many come back.'

'I'm sorry to hear that,' I said.

'We've lost three dogs this month,' Harold added. 'The women are scared for their young kids, and the young fellas who fish down there have been stalked a bit too.'

Harold and I walked around to the back of his place with another young lad to check out the surrounds. The creek was Harold's backyard – about three metres from his doorstep was the bank leading down to the water, and in between the two stretched an unfenced patch of grass with a kids' plastic playground, basketball ring and sprinkler, which I imagined Harold's grandkids played around to cool off. It was a recipe for disaster.

'Harold, can you show me how big you think this croc's head is?'

He pointed to me. 'The size of your torso.'

The young fella nodded in agreement. 'Yeah, when I saw him out of the water last year his head was at least a metre.'

The reports were all the same: this was a bloody big croc.

Harold confirmed that he was happy for us to film everything, so I went home, locked in *60 Minutes* and returned to Peppi a week later with Willow. I'd just got a new land cruiser, so we took it for a burn and navigated the unsealed roads out to Peppi. We kept an eye out for feral pigs on the way to use as bait. There weren't many around, but we did spot a dingo on the edge of the scrub near the road.

'Shit, take a look at that thing,' Willow said, scrunching up his face.

The right side of the dingo's face had opened up and a cyst the size of a softball was protruding from it. The wound was bloody and infected, and the flesh was hanging from the dingo's face. We waited in the car and watched as it staggered across the road in front of us. It was half-dead, the poor thing.

'That is so messed up,' Willow said. 'Is it diseased or what, Matty?'

I shook my head. 'I don't know, but I think we need to put the poor bastard out of his misery. He's in a hell of a lot of pain and there is no saving him.'

'Righto.' Without any more talk Willow got out of the

car, pulled out his 44-Desert Eagle and shot the dingo in one hit. He walked over, picked it up by its legs and dragged it off into the bushes, hidden away to lay to rest.

'That dingo looked like it was out of an alien movie,' I said to Willow as we drove off. 'I've never seen something so mangled. Good thing it's at peace now.'

We managed to find two pigs for bait just before we reached Peppi, arriving mid-afternoon. We drove straight to the creek bed. I was hoping we'd find any trace of the croc, so I could show Willow what we were up against.

'Flipping hell, Matty, check this out.'

There, clear as day, was a thumping crocodile slide mark stamped into the mud. There was a crocodile footprint too. It was at least six times the size of Willow's hand and the markings were noticeably bigger than the tracks left by my 17-foot pet croc, Tripod. There was no denying we had a monster on our hands. We put the bait near the slide marks and set up a couple more cameras in the trees. I caught myself looking over my shoulder every now and then, which I don't often do, but an animal of that size could swallow me whole. I decided not to put a trap out because I wanted to get footage of what we were dealing with first, so we set up the usual cameras to get some intel.

The location was not where we would normally catch a croc; it was in a township, not in the middle of Woop Woop, so we even had access to wi-fi. This meant that our sensor cameras could send live notifications and pictures to Willow's phone every time there was movement.

His phone started going nuts that afternoon when we were back at Harold's place, but it was a false alarm. We watched as a couple of smaller 12-foot crocs entered the area to suss the bait out. While we waited, Harold took us to the community's workshop and salvage yard to get started on building the trap.

'Are you kidding?!' I exclaimed, looking around the workshop. 'You've got everything here that we need to make the trap. This makes things a hell of a lot easier.'

The workshop was about 200 metres from the creek and was stocked with a mountain of steel, old cattle pens, thick mesh and fencing: too much to choose from, really. Every now and then, Willow's phone pinged with a notification about movement down at the creek, but nothing worth taking notice of.

'Still no sign of the big boy, Harold,' I said.

'Oh, the *Baru* is in there, just give him time and he'll show himself,' he said.

'Why don't we work here over the next week welding up the traps and in that time hopefully we'll get some good footage,' suggested Willow, and I agreed.

Aboriginal people call the saltwater crocodile *Baru*, which means 'crocodile's ancestor'. Many local people in Peppi hold crocodiles as their totem and are responsible for looking after them, so harming one in any way would not be acceptable. Even if the croc ate a person, the local people still wouldn't want the animal shot, and that's why they were keen for me to safely relocate it.

We based ourselves at Elizabeth Downs Station, which was only an hour's drive to get to Peppi each day. The welding was more work than we had anticipated but we built a bloody good trap door, and I already had a couple of traps in Darwin that I planned on bringing back to use as well.

Each morning Willow and I rebaited near the creek, then got to work. The sensor cameras continued to reveal that there were several crocs in the area – and big ones at that – but none big enough to wow me and make me think it was the one we were after.

Once we finished welding the main trap, we headed back to Darwin and I let Nick know that we were ready for the *60 Minutes* crew to arrive. Then I drove back to Peppi ahead of the shoot to set up the big panel trap, using old pens from cattle yards and other large sturdy pieces of steel, which can be welded together to create a trap that's more like an enclosure, with a door that releases when the bait is pulled on. This time Jono came along to help me erect the trap, tying up the trigger rope with the bait attached on one end and the trap door on the other. This meant there would be no mucking around once the camera crew arrived.

'There are some big marks over here, Matt, check it out.' Jono tiptoed around the trap's steel panels and pointed to the bank on the opposite side of the river. There was a similar-sized slide mark to the one Willow and I had seen a few weeks earlier along the bank.

I nodded. 'I reckon we've seen just about every croc in the area on camera except the big one, but he's leaving a good trail for us.'

Setting up the trap was a mission, but we got there in the end and then booted back to Darwin.

The cars were packed, the traps were stacked and Willow, Jono and I were up early the next day to greet the small *60 Minutes* crew from Sydney. After a briefing and a lot of questions, the crew hit the road for the four-hour drive. I flew out with Pete Stefanovic, Jono and Benny the cameraman to have a yarn and get a feel for the story.

'As you've heard, there's been a ton of reports of crocs getting too close for comfort, so it's our job to go in and move them out,' I told them. 'Unfortunately, we can't relocate these ones back into the wild elsewhere because they're deemed as "problem animals". If we catch them and I can't get them into the local farm, I'll take them back to my joint and build a pen to keep them safe there.'

We made a quick stop at my bush shack and visited the lagoon that backs onto it. I got Pete out on the lagoon in the airboat with me and some of my crocs that I work with regularly. I wanted to give him some hands-on croc experience before the real deal, but I don't think the poor bloke knew what he was getting into.

'All right, Pete, jump off here and come say hello to Bone Cruncher,' I said, parking the airboat along the bank.

'What, me get down there WITH you?' he asked, uncertainly.

'Yep, that's the one.'

Hesitantly, he hopped onto the ground and stood close beside me as I fended off Bone Cruncher, a 14-foot resident female croc.

'So, Pete, the biggest thing when a crocodile is coming at you is to always make sure you've got an exit. You've got a tree behind you now, so just be aware of that, and always check your surroundings while you're moving about.'

Pete shuffled from foot to foot, looking around. 'Matt, I just am not sure exactly what to say right now. There's nothing between us and this apex predator but a stick.'

'Correct,' I confirmed. 'But in this particular situation we've got the advantage. We're up high on a slope so we've just got to make sure we stay out of the kill zone and we've got nothing to worry about.'

Pete didn't seem overly convinced but we finished feeding Bone Cruncher and I was glad he got a taster of what was in store out at Peppi. I also made sure we stopped by Tripod's pen on the way back to the chopper.

'Pete, please meet Tripod. Tripod, this is Pete. Tripod, please don't eat Pete.'

Pete let out a nervous laugh.

'I can't quite believe what I'm seeing right now to be honest,' he said to me as we got back into the air.

'Mate, you ain't seen nothing yet,' I said.

•

Just outside of Peppi, we spotted a good mob of wild pigs from the chopper, so I landed us and shut the machine down. We needed a few pigs as bait – one for the big panel trap and three more for the smaller cage traps I planned on slinging into other areas of the creek. We were upwind, so the pigs couldn't smell or hear us, and we continued to creep up as they moved about on a patch of grass at the edge of a water channel. Slowly, we crept forward, hearing the pigs' wallowing getting louder and louder. All of a sudden, a big boar noticed us and started storming straight at me, so I let my first shot off.

The pigs began scattering everywhere. I let a few more rounds go and in the flurry of bullets I downed four more pigs. We dragged them back to the chopper and tied them up, ready to sling out. I couldn't manage to lift them all, so I took the legs off one of them. I dropped the legs off, along with Jono, Pete and Benny, then returned for the rest of the hogs.

Once everyone had arrived at the creek, I introduced Pete to Harold. After some brief hellos Pete got Harold's take on it all.

'How scared are you?' Pete asked him.

'Very scared, very concerned,' Harold replied.

'Do you think it could take someone?' Pete continued.

'Yes, that possibility is real. It's scary,' he said. 'There are a few crocs here we would like moved out, but one of them is really no good.'

I explained to Pete that we would also be setting up a couple of smaller cage traps to capture the crocs that were lurking around on local sacred sites used for men's business. Aside from local Aboriginal men, no one else is allowed to visit these areas.

'This will be the first time a white man has ever visited these areas,' I explained to camera. This illustrated more than anything how desperate the locals were to have these problem crocs caught and moved out. 'Harold has asked me to place two traps in this particular spot in an attempt to move out a couple of the smaller crocs who have been hassling the local men.'

I baited and set two of the traps into the area, but we were forbidden to film any of it.

Then there were two more cage traps to bait and put down the other end of the creek, near a swimming hole. Willow baited the first trap while I chucked a pig leg up the back of the second trap and invited Pete to lend a hand.

'Now the pig leg is in there, we have to crawl into the back of the cage and secure it,' I said to him.

'Who's doing that?' Pete asked.

'YOU,' I told him.

A smile edged onto his face. He got down on his hands and knees.

'Don't shut that gate on me,' he said.

'No, no, I won't,' I reassured him, with a twinkle in my eye.

So Pete crawled into the trap and of course I let the gate down immediately, locking him inside.

'Yep, the trap works,' I joked.

There was leftover bait at the back from weeks before, so it stunk like all buggery in there. Pete dry-retched but handled it like a trooper, laughing it off. He was proving to be pretty easy-going and adaptable.

Once the remaining cage traps were baited, I slung them into place and explained the difference between the two types of traps.

'The large panel traps are for your 15-foot-plus crocs and these cage traps are for your smaller ones. Now let's go set up the big one.'

Willow showed Pete some of the markings on our way over to the main trap. 'See the marks here? That's his hands and that's his claws. These are fresh tracks left just a couple of days ago, I'd say.'

'Yeah, right, that is a big animal. It looks like a dinosaur print,' Pete observed. Then he fixed his attention on something else. 'What's that? Is that a gun in your pocket?' he asked, pointing to the shiny gold Desert Eagle sticking out of Willow's pants. I'm sure he was half taking the mickey out of him.

Willow defended his case. 'Yeah, mate, you need one of these out here. I've never had to use it before but it's just in case a big fella gets a hold of your leg.'

'The man with the golden gun,' Pete proclaimed, and Jono and I had a laugh.

Willow shrugged. 'I've copped a lot of slack about it, but I bet the lads won't tease me if I ever had to use it.'

'Fair enough, mate,' Pete said politely.

I took Pete through the ins and outs of catching a

crocodile, and the mechanics of the large panel trap, showing him how to tie a pig to the trigger rope. His face lit up as I demonstrated to him how to navigate everything. I imagine it was all pretty fascinating for a city lad.

The area the trap was erected in was a perfect little dam off to the side of the main creek; the entrance was exactly the right size to fit the big trap door.

We walked around the upper rows of the panels, making sure everything was tied up tight enough. Then we climbed onto the outside of the trap to make our way back onto dry land. Pete lost his footing a bit moving about.

'DO NOT fall back, whatever you do,' I warned him. 'There's a good chance the croc is lying right there.'

Pete understood, and held on tighter. I lifted the trap door up with the help of everyone and set the trigger rope. We had the trap set and ready for action by the afternoon.

'The waiting game begins, guys,' I told them. 'I'll be surprised if we don't catch a croc in one of the traps straight-up, given the time of year. In the dry season, crocs go dormant and don't eat as much, but now that it's the build-up to the wet season they've started mating and are very hungry, very horny and more aggressive.'

I flew back to Elizabeth Downs Station with Pete and Benny, while the others drove. We all crashed around the outside table with a beer in hand.

Ping, ping, ping!

Willow's phone started going nuts. He passed it around for us to have a closer look, and we saw footage of big splashes and pig guts flying about the place: the trap was alive with activity. This went on for a while and then the trap door finally dropped down at 9 p.m., securing something inside.

'Let's hope our guy is in there,' I said. 'It'll be an early start tomorrow – you mob will get trucking at 5.30 in the cars to get to the trap at first light. And we won't be far behind in the chopper.'

The next morning the anticipation was high, but we were met with disappointment. There was nothing in the trap. I scouted the area and could see where the croc had got out by the tracks that went from the water's edge, up over the patch of dry land and though a gap in one of the cattle pens. Willow's footage showed a decent-sized croc but, judging by the size of the gap in the pen, it couldn't have been bigger than 15 feet. Harold was keen for us to catch and move anything larger than 14 feet, so I reinforced the panels with mesh to keep anything and everything inside the trap's walls. We put more pig meat on the trigger and were done by 10 o'clock that morning. There was nothing else we could do, so we drove back to Lizzy Downs.

We had just sat down to lunch when Willow's phone ran riot again. Less than two hours after we'd left, the croc had gone in and set the trap off. We scoffed down our food and jumped in the car for another hour-long trip.

We convoyed all the way back to Peppi and pulled the croc out. The animal was about 15 foot and painfully malnourished. Given that he was a hungry croc and would keep on causing headaches, we had to move him along.

'This one can go straight to the farm, Willow,' I instructed.

'Roger.'

We pulled him out and Willow arranged for one of the workers from the croc farm to bring a truck and drive him to Darwin.

The next part was the same – reset, rebait, repeat. Then we returned to the station.

We were sitting around the campfire watching the sun set over the Lizzy Downs floodplains and spinning yarns about the day when Willow came outside and let us know we had another croc.

'Another early start, team,' I told them. 'The trap door is down, and we've got a big animal in there.'

It's quite unique seeing two big crocs going into the same trap within 24 hours of each other. Even after the trap door dropped down, the croc continued to eat an entire pig and didn't at all seem fazed that he was locked up. The croc was completely motivated by food, another hungry animal in kill mode.

We went to bed on a high, eager to wake. The crew hit the road and the usual suspects went with me in the chopper at first light. Pete and I spoke to camera while Benny filmed us and got some sweeping scenery shots. I flew over the trap to see a croc resting on the water's surface.

'He's got a big head on him but still doesn't match the mammoth description I've been given,' I said to camera.

We landed and walked down to the trap nice and quietly and waited for the rest of the crew to rock up with the trailer, mattresses, harpoons and sedative drugs. Then we got into it. I poked around, and the croc roared about. There wasn't much room to move inside the pen, so Benny was sitting up on the rail filming. The croc hurled out and hit the rail halfway up, right at Benny's feet. The cameraman lost his balance and wobbled back and forth, like a seesaw. I was already in full flight towards him, ready to harpoon the croc or lure it towards me, before Benny fell right on top of it.

But, by a stroke of absolute luck, Benny's balance threw him ever so slightly backwards and he fell outside of the trap, landing amongst the spikey pandan plants and loose logs. He had prickles, twigs and mud all over him, but to his credit he got right back up on the railing and continued filming Pete and me, who were walking on the outskirts of the dam within the trap. I secured the harpoon line in the croc, to bring its head above the water. I pulled it in as it put up a fight, swimming about and resisting me. Without warning Pete stumbled backwards, looking at me with confusion.

'Shit, Pete, move! Jump up on that railing!'

Pete shot up immediately. The dam's edge must have been underhung in the exact spot where Pete was standing. The croc was pushing its nose up from underneath Pete, trying to break free. Pete was one lucky bastard because that croc could have very easily broken that sandy barrier and snapped his feet off! The croc resurfaced in the shallow water, hurling itself onto the air, trying to snap on anything and everything.

'Whoa, he's a nice strong animal, lads!' I called out.

It took a fair while to get the croc out of the waterhole, but we got there eventually and Jono put a head rope on him. Willow opened up the panel traps and we had everything ready to get the beast out.

By this time the whole community had gathered around to see what was going on. The day before we'd left pretty quietly, but now the word had got around, we had the local coppers, nurses, teachers, store owners and others young and old watching us.

I didn't realise at the time, but *60 Minutes* had worked with my manager, Nick, to secretly fly my mum up from Adelaide to surprise me for the segment. Mum had raised me in the country and taught me a lot about living off the land and working with animals, but in the 20 years of me living up north she had never seen me catch a croc in person. So, right in the middle of it all, mid-harpooning and knee-deep in water I turned around to see my old girl standing there, looking at me with complete pride. I beamed back at her. That small moment meant a lot to me and to her.

As the croc catch unfolded, the main camera was on me while a second camera was on Mum, who was getting asked to commentate. Each time I looked over at her she smiled: she was loving every minute of it.

At one point I heard her say, 'He should know what he's doing by now, so if he screws up it's his own bloody fault.'

'Thanks, Mum!' I called back to her, laughing.

The croc kept retreating to the bottom of the trap and there was only really Willow, Jono, Pete and me there to muscle the croc out. I needed to pull him up enough to get the needle with the drugs in him.

'Go and grab the car, unhitch the trailer and we'll try and winch him out,' I said to Willow.

There was a steep embankment above where we were, so the car could have rolled in a heartbeat, but Willow navigated it well, and reached us safely. I usually don't like using a winch because it's too slow for my liking, but we didn't have another option in this case. I managed to attach the winch line to the croc, no worries.

Each time Willow activated the winch to pull, we'd tug on the line, lifting the croc's jaw so it didn't get caught on anything. I was trying to get the croc out as quickly as possible because it was getting hot and I wanted to avoid a build-up of lactic acid in the croc's body, which can be life-threatening. As Willow reversed the car up the hill, the wheels began to spin on the spot, getting bogged in the loose sand. He slammed his foot down and the car hopped backwards and into a pile of star pickets, puncturing a tyre.

Ya kidding me, I thought but I held my tongue. There was no time for a blue.

I had to get all the lads on the end of the rope still attached to the croc as well as some young strong Aboriginal blokes to keep holding it taut, while I helped Willow replace the tyre and reverse up the hill with the croc in tow. One thing's for sure, catching crocs is never smooth sailing.

We finally hauled him out onto the embankment, got a needle into his tail and put hessian over his eyes to calm him down. I let him sit for half an hour in the shade and then it was time to get him on the trailer.

Ten local Aboriginal ladies appeared out of nowhere and came down close to the car and began wailing for their totem. I didn't understand what they were saying, but they were crying and sounded like they were in pain. I had aimed on creating next to no commotion, but I wasn't doing a very good job at it. Harold consoled the ladies and assured me it was okay to carry on.

'They are sad to see him leave but they know it is the right thing, and they are blessing him and wishing him a good journey in the future,' Harold told me.

We hooked the car back to the trailer at the top of the embankment. The croc was up on the flat, ready to go. Jono got the mattress prepped and wet down the croc because it was a pretty warm day. We kept his head visible as well, so we could monitor his breathing. When a croc is anaesthetised, you have to watch the animal's nostrils, ensuring they shut every minute or so at least.

At this point, I pulled Harold aside to give him my thoughts. 'I still don't know if this is the croc you're after.'

Yes, the croc was a big croc at 16-and-a-half feet, but it wasn't the 20-foot giant they'd been talking about.

'I'm not sure either, Matty,' he replied.

'Well, do you want me to set the trap again tomorrow? We got two big crocs in two days, so it's just a matter of time, really. I guarantee you the next one will be a thumper.'

But because of all the upset and commotion that the croc-catching had caused within the community, Harold called the search off for good.

We pulled the trap down and packed it up while the croc continued to rest under the tree. I slung everything else back into the workshop and onto our equipment trailer, and sent Willow and Jono, along with the producer and the second cameraman, back in the vehicle to take the croc back to Lizzy Downs. It was just me, Mum and Pete left.

'Come on,' I said to them. 'Let's go for a cheeky fish on the flight back to the station.'

We flew over a waterhole called Wilson's, famous for an 18-foot croc named Wilson that was pulled out of the area 10 years earlier. Wilson's is a shaded tropical oasis full of life, including massive barramundi. Mum had never caught a barra before, so I was hoping for a good session.

'Come on, old girl, flick it in there!' I said.

She was blessed with beginner's luck, and on her first cast she hooked onto a big one. Pulling it in with all her might, she was struggling with the fish as it darted around.

'Keep pulling, Mum!' I shouted. 'Do you want a hand?'

'Not a chance!' she bit back, jokingly. 'You're not taking any of the glory!'

The fish finally tired out after 10 minutes of reeling and repositioning, and she pulled it up.

'No way! Mum, it's a stonker! Hang on, stay here.'

I bolted to the chopper and found the measuring tape.

'Okay, bets are on. Pete, what do you reckon?'

'Ninety centimetres,' he said.

'Mum?'

She shrugged. 'Hmmm, no idea. Very big is all I've got.'

'Righto, I'm going for a metre!' I laid out the tape and, I kid you not, the old girl bagged a 104-centimetre-long barra on her first ever cast during her first ever barra expedition.

'I don't believe it! At least we have dinner sorted now!' I said.

We caught a couple more big fish, and even Pete caught one around the 90-cm mark. We were stoked with our efforts and booted back to Lizzy Downs after our perfect little fishing outing.

Pete interviewed Mum and me that night as the sun set behind the cathedral termite mounds. It was nice hearing her reflect on the relationship we have and the adventures and misadventures that we've shared along the way.

'Well, the fruit definitely doesn't fall far from the tree, does it?' he remarked after the interview.

There was no denying me and my old girl have the same love of wildlife and zest for adventure. There aren't too many mums out there who would encourage their son to catch one of the deadliest animals in the world, but she thinks it's all a bit of fun and doesn't see what the fuss is all about. She'd be out there doing the same as me if she were younger!

We took the second croc to my neighbour's place near Dundee and spent a few days working around the clock to build a pen at the back of his joint to keep the croc out of harm's way. The cros still lives there today. I had a ball with Pete and the crew, and the *60 Minutes* segment turned out mint.

•

Every now and then I would still think about Peppi and wonder if that monster was a myth or not. And then, about a month after the *60 Minutes* episode went to air, I received a call from a coroner in Katherine.

'Is this Matt Wright?'

'Roger.'

'G'day, mate,' she said. 'I'm from the Katherine Police and we're conducting an investigation. I'm hoping to ask you a few questions, if that's okay?'

'Sure thing,' I replied.

'Have you been catching crocodiles around Peppimenarti recently?'

'Yes, about five weeks ago I removed two.'

'How many did you see in the area?'

'There's a few around there. How come?'

'Unfortunately, we've just lost a local down there. He's been taken by a crocodile.'

'You're kidding me.' My heart sank. I knew straight away that we definitely hadn't caught the croc we were after.

'Wish I was.'

'Thank you for letting me know. I'll have a chat to the locals and see if they want me to come back again,' I said.

Sadly, Harold and Captain, another senior traditional owner, had passed away from health-related issues soon after that attack. When I found out, I realised that's why I hadn't heard from anyone in the community.

I would still like to go back to Peppi one day – that's if the locals wanted me to – and see if I can catch the cunning croc, because I would hate for him to take any more innocent lives.

11

Outback Wrangler, season three

When preproduction for season three of *Outback Wrangler* came around we began planning and working through our stories, and one of the biggest things we wanted to incorporate was more educational information about crocodiles. I work with crocodiles every day and know a lot about the animal. But I haven't learnt everything I know from books – it has come from my interactions with the animals over the past 20 years.

When I talk about crocodiles on the show, a lot of what I say is observational commentary as opposed to hard-hitting facts. The knowledge and insight I have is pretty unique because I live and breathe the animal in the wild, and it works on *Wrangler*, but my theoretical and scientific understanding of crocodiles could do with some work.

In my younger croc-catching years I knew how to read and catch a croc better than anyone. I never felt the need to learn more, because that's all I cared about back then.

I was a croc catcher, not a croc expert. Of course, I've picked up a hell of a lot of information over the years working alongside scientists in the field, but as I do more TV shows and media interviews the more I am asked specialist questions.

During an interview a couple of years ago, when I was promoting season two of *Outback Wrangler*, I was talking about a crocodile's tail and the scute-marking system we use to identify crocs.

The presenter interrupted me mid-discussion. 'Sorry, Matt, and what exactly is a scute?'

'A scute, I guess, is similar to a hard bit of cartilage covered in skin,' I said.

My answer didn't quite cut the mustard and the presenter prompted me some more.

'And a more scientific explanation?'

I just sat there without a clue in the world and made a joke about how I catch crocs, not study them, and the audience laughed along with me. I went home that night and googled 'scutes' and it came up with 'Scutes are the keratinous sheathes that cover the osteoderms'. I remember thinking, *Shit. I do need to learn more about the inner workings of these animals, especially if people are referring to me as a 'croc expert'.*

So educating myself in the lead-up to *Wrangler* season three was a big focus, not just for the show but for the publicity tour that would follow. That way, I could be in a position to go into greater scientific detail if I was asked.

I lived on the net and read a few books for a good couple of months, trawling information, and called Webby every now and then to validate things.

I've always spent a lot of time around Darwin-based reptile scientist Professor Grahame 'Webby' Webb. Given that we're both locals and work closely with crocodiles in our respective fields, we often find ourselves at presentations, talks and sometimes out in the field together, talking all things crocodile. Grahame began researching crocs in the late 1960s, and in my opinion, he is the world's leading authority on croc research and management.

And just before we began filming for *Wrangler*, I was invited to co-host an event with Webby at Charles Darwin University, where I got the opportunity to listen to his insights more than ever before, taking notes and picking his brain when I found something interesting. No matter how much you know about a topic, there is always something new to learn, and I loved every minute of getting to know crocodiles even better than before. And even after studying for a few months and continuing to research regularly to this day, there is so much out there for me still to learn and so much that all of us are yet to discover about this prehistoric predator.

I wanted to incorporate more science into what we do in future shows, particularly with tracking devices to learn more about crocodiles' territorial behaviours and whether they do have a homing instinct, as is often thought.

From my experience and recent study of the animal, here

are ten things that I find interesting, which are less commonly known:

- The length of a croc can be calculated by multiplying the length of their head by seven.
- Crocs' osteoderms (located on their back), are like big solar panels. A croc can cook to death if it's in the sun for too long.
- Crocs swallow stones to grind down food in their tummy and cough up big fur balls from eating wild pigs.
- Crocs are good climbers and can get up extremely steep surfaces.
- Crocs can't die of biological causes. (See page 151 for explanation.)
- Their eyes, ears and nostrils are all located on the top of their head.
- They have a highly acidic tummy, so they can quickly digest bones, horns and hooves.
- The saying 'crocodile tears' is true! Crocs produce tears, but it's because of swallowing air not crying.
- Crocs open their jaws to cool themselves because they don't have sweat glands.
- The muscles that open their jaws have little strength, hence why gaffer tape does the trick for me!

By the time filming arrived for *Outback Wrangler* season three, I was geared up with info and ready to weave new facts and information into our adventures. If you watch the shows, you'll see that info incorporated mostly through onscreen pop-ups, and the voiceover. I tried to tie things into the action where possible, but the reality is that the moment you have a croc in front of you, you're focused intently on catching the animal and not getting chewed, rather than turning to the camera and going on about how a croc can swim up to 15 km per hour. That's not really a priority in a high-risk situation. Nevertheless, I managed to throw in bits and pieces where I could. It was more informative than previous seasons, but there is still room for improvement when season four comes around, that's for sure.

•

We had eight episodes in season three of *Outback Wrangler*, all shot around the Top End. Two of the most memorable and demanding episodes were at Adelaide River Station and Moroak Station. We shot these episodes in tandem, which wasn't evident in the final cut of the show. The episodes aired as two stand-alone events, when in fact they were very much intertwined. This was not at all planned, especially given the large geographical distance between the two locations – Adelaide River is 130 kilometres south of Darwin, while Moroak is 600 kilometres southeast of Darwin, next to the Roper River. But in an unexpected series of events, I ended up having to catch crocs in the two locations at pretty much the same time, which was a mission to say the least.

My mate Mick Jacobi manages Adelaide River Station and had been on my case for years to get out there and catch, according to him, 'the biggest croc in the Territory'. I finally agreed to do it because it was taking more and more cattle from his property.

And then a friend of a friend reached out to me about going to Moroak to relocate a problem crocodile after a couple of incidents. The owner of Moroak Station is a lad by the name of Simon Hoar, and he and his wife and their four boys under the age of six moved there not long ago. The homestead is so close to the river that you can cast a fishing line and catch a barra from the front porch.

It's a pretty setting, but then crocs started popping up on the front lawn and humbugging the family while they were fishing. They put up fencing to keep the crocs away, but there was one big fella that kept coming back. It got to the point where, the moment the family ventured beyond the fence or out on their boat for the day, the croc would have a crack at them.

Jono and I, along with my dog Naish, made the long six-hour drive to Moroak. We offloaded our traps and gear and then planned to hit the sack as we had an early start the next morning. We just wanted to get a couple of pigs, set the cameras and boot straight back to Darwin, because the crew weren't arriving for another couple of weeks and all we needed for now was some insight into where the crocs were hanging out.

The next morning we drove around for an hour trying to find a pig. I'm used to spotting one from the air while flying a chopper, and it was the first time in a long time I'd had to look for one from the ground.

'This is hard yakka, Jonsy. I don't know how we're going to do this, especially because I'm not familiar with the country around here.'

'Yeah, I'm with you,' Jono agreed.

We came across an old cattle yard and finally heard and saw some movement in the bushes.

'There, Matty!' Jono called.

Naish must have heard him, and leapt from the tray, towards the noise. But it wasn't pigs, it was a couple of wallabies. They jumped out across the open plains.

'Oh noooo,' I said, stalling the car and flinging the door open. 'Naish!' I screamed, but she was gone, chasing the wallabies through the bushes. She had no chance of catching them but was obsessed with them, and had been ever since she was a pup.

'That's no good, Jonsy. We're going to have Buckley's chance of finding her again, especially without a chopper.'

We did a few bog laps, but we couldn't see her, as I expected.

'There's not much we can do right now, so let's drive around until we get a pig, set them along the banks with the cameras, and when the boys are back from mustering I'll ask Simon to borrow a chopper,' I said.

'Okay, sounds good,' Jono replied. 'Sorry about yelling out, mate. I didn't think.'

'All good. What will be will be, I guess,' I said, praying that I hadn't lost Naish.

•

It was 2 p.m. We'd found some pigs, set the cameras and I had my hands on a chopper. Two hours, and a lot of money wasted in fuel later, I still couldn't see Naish anywhere. We covered kilometres and kilometres from the air, scoping anywhere that looked like a possibility. Feeling completely defeated and heartbroken, I started flying back.

'We can't sleep at home tonight, Jonsy,' I said. 'I want to take the swags in the back of the car and sleep out in the old cattle yard where we lost her, in case she makes her way back.'

'Roger. I was going to suggest the same thing.'

About five kilometres from the cattle yard, I saw a small clearing with bushes scattered around just to the side of the dirt road we'd driven down earlier that day, and there, lying next to one of the bushes, was a white speck.

'No way, I think that's her.'

I dropped the chopper and hooked in to land. And there was Naish, curled up in the shade of a bush, totally exhausted. She couldn't get up, but she was wagging her tail and smiling. I ran towards her and smothered her in kisses and hugs. God, I was relieved. And tucked underneath a shrub next to her was a male dingo. He was the most placid fella, he didn't even get up to come at me, he just sat there. I'd never seen anything like it.

Jono came in behind me. 'How funny is that! Naish has found herself a fling out here!' he joked.

'I can't believe he's just sitting there, with us here. Mate, can you get the sat phone and ask the guys to come fetch her in the ute?'

'Roger,' said Jono, and went off to make the call.

'Come on, girl, come sit in the chopper with me and have some water before the ute arrives. Say goodbye to your mate.'

I carried Naish to the chopper, sitting down with her in the back seat. I turned around and saw that the dingo had followed me to the chopper. It jumped in.

'I actually can't believe it, it's like he's domesticated!' I said.

The dingo sat there with us until the guys came in the ute to pick up Naish and we parted ways with the dingo. I felt bad leaving him behind, but he was happy and healthy, and I was sure he would be okay.

•

Two weeks later Jono, Ash and I flew back out to Moroak to get things ready for the rest of the camera crew, who would be landing in Darwin two days later. On the way, we stopped by Adelaide River Station and set up a large panel trap with Mick's help. I figured we would get a croc trap going there first and test the waters before heading to Moroak to get things sorted properly there. Things were organised quick-smart with Mick and we took to the skies early arvo en route to our final destination at Moroak.

We flew around where we dropped the pigs a few weeks earlier to have a look at what was going on. We had with us four big cage traps, which we placed down first and then got stuck into setting up the smaller panel traps in two key locations we'd chosen based on croc activity from our camera footage.

Lots of little crocs and two decent-sized animals cruised along the waterway while we were setting the traps.

'This place is full of them!' Jono commented.

'Yeah, it is,' I said. 'We're not going to have trouble getting one in there, but it's going to be a headache if we keep catching the wrong one!'

My mate Munro happened to be mustering in the area, so he flew in to lend a hand reinforcing the trap. The boys double-tied the panels together while I set up the trigger rope. I turned around to check on their progress and there was Munro, all five foot seven of him, on the *outside* of the trap, up to his neck in the water.

'Christ, Munro, get in here now!'

He was bloody lucky his leg didn't get chewed; we'd seen so many big animals swimming past only metres from where he was.

Munro scampered up the trap and jumped inside it. 'Yeah crap, sorry mate, I had a bit of a brain fart there.'

'YA RECKON?!' Jono said.

The day was done and it was time for us to set up camp. We could have stayed at the homestead but it was dry season, and we'd found a spot near a crystal-clear shallow creek where we set up an epic little site with chairs, tents and swags. It was a camping paradise.

•

The next morning, after campfire baked beans and crusty bread for breakfast, I flew with Jono over the trap. We saw a heap of dirty water and, sure enough, a big crocodile.

'Oh shit,' I said. 'We've caught one within two days of setting it.'

It wasn't what I expected or wanted. We were trying to save money, so we didn't have the camera crew. They were all still in Darwin because we thought it would take a few days at least to set the traps and lure the crocs in.

'Hmmm, bit of a problem,' I said to Jono.

I flew higher to 2000 feet to get service to message Willow to get the camera crew and boot straight out as soon as possible because we had an animal in the trap already. As I got bars on my phone a message came through from Mick over at Mount Bundy Station: *Croc in the trap*.

'Oh, ya kidding. Jono, we've got one at Mount Bundy as well!' I said. 'The camera crew arrive in Darwin today, so I'm thinking we leave this guy here and fly to Adelaide River, meet the crew there first and film that one.'

'He's only just got in there and he's in the shade, so he'll be fine,' Jono agreed.

Willow was now across the plan, had picked up the remaining crew members and was driving southbound to Adelaide River Station.

'I still can't believe we already caught the croc, I didn't even bait the trap properly!' I said.

I'd put a bit of pig up on the rail of the trap to entice the croc in so we could get some footage of the size we were dealing with before the camera crew arrived, but the croc must have swam in and knocked the gate down in the process.

We flew over the croc in the trap to suss it out on our way to the Adelaide River homestead, and confirmed Mick's size misjudgement.

'Is it the big one we're after?' he asked, the moment I walked in the kitchen door.

'Well, it's big, mate, but I hate to break it to you, I don't think it's the 20-foot monster you've been talking about.'

'Yeah, righto,' he replied. 'Well it's probably not the one we're after then.'

Mick was married to the idea of this supposed 'monster'. I'd been wrong in the past so a small part of me thought there could be a bigger croc out there, but I doubted it.

'Mate, you're a small fella, so I think your point of reference is a bit off!' I joked. 'You think everything is big, like a Chihuahua thinking a kelpie is a Great Dane!'

'Hey, hey, come on now. I'm telling you it is, I've seen it fair and square,' he argued.

'Righto, well, let's get this one out tomorrow morning and see what else shows itself after that,' I said.

The crew arrived that night, along with Willow's dad, Robert, who brought a trailer, and Tommy Nichols from NT Parks and Wildlife, who brought the drugs for the croc. I was mentally drained but pleased I'd managed to align all of the moving parts and people.

At dawn, I flew the chopper by myself to check on the croc. I wanted to ensure everything was kosher before filming. I landed and I had a look over the trap. The water was muddy, but there wasn't much in there for the croc to hide in.

No croc. He'd managed to squeeze out through the gaps in the bars.

'Shit.' I pulled the motion sensors off the trap so I could see exactly what had happened and flew back to the homestead. Everyone was up and buzzing, ready for the first day. All I could think was, *What a waste of time, we could be at Moroak pulling the other croc out and here we are for nothing.*

'Do you want the good news or the bad news?' I said as I walked through the kitchen door.

'What?' everyone asked.

'Bad news is the croc is gone. Good news is there wasn't a big struggle from the looks of things, so we haven't scared him off and he's likely to come back in the next day or two.

But we have to reinforce the trap, so he doesn't get out. And I can tell you one thing for sure, Mick, he's certainly no beast because he's managed to slip through the unmeshed rails. So, I'm guessing he's around the 15-foot mark, still a big croc, but not a next-level mammoth.'

Everyone looked at me like, 'Are you for real?!' but I rousted everyone up and we got going.

'Come on, you lot, the croc isn't going to catch itself, and we all like a challenge, so let's get moving!' I said light-heartedly.

We went back out to the trap and strapped some big melaleuca branches to the rails to make the gaps smaller.

'Well, that didn't go to plan, guys, sorry about that,' I said.

Jono, Ash, Dan and I then flew over to Moroak to check on the other croc, while Tommy and Robert went home to Darwin, defeated. The rest of the crew were going to drive from Adelaide River to Moroak, and wouldn't be getting in until dark.

Holy hell, did the croc in the Moroak trap go ballistic when we arrived. He'd found a little gap at the bottom of the embankment where the ground was uneven and started wedging his nose under it, lifting the trap up and bending the mesh outwards, trying to escape. His tail thrashed around like a whip, and he was death-rolling every now and then, causing the trap to wobble about.

I walked to one side of the trap and pulled a patch of mesh off. I poked a stick through the gap between the rails, enticing the croc towards me. He came straight over and shoved his snout through the gap.

'Rope, quick Jono!' I looped the rope over his head and pushed him back inside, making sure my hands didn't get chomped in the process. I managed to pull him back inside with a head rope attached.

I thought I had him but then, without warning, the croc darted for the gap he'd made under the trap and pulled me straight into the one-metre-deep water in the trap alongside him. Everyone stopped filming, dropped their gear and jumped up on the horizontal rails of the trap to pull me out, yelling all sorts. I thought I was dead meat; I honestly thought that was it for me in that moment. But, luckily for me, the croc had clawed so hard under the gap trying to escape that he had wedged himself in there and couldn't back out to eat me. His tail thrashed me around for a bit, and I felt like I was getting dumped by waves at the beach, but I eventually made it over the rails.

'Matty, you good?' Willow asked.

'Yeah guys, shit, that was close. Don't worry about me, let's pull him back out, otherwise we'll lose him as well and that'll be two crocs in two days and I'm not having that.'

It was all hands on deck to secure the animal and get him out of the trap.

'He's decent, just under 16 foot, I reckon. Call Simon and get him to bring his buggy down to pull the croc up the steep bank,' I said to Willow.

Simon arrived and was happy. 'That's definitely one of

the crocs we're after,' he confirmed. 'I've seen him out of the water before, he's one of the culprits for sure.'

Willow got him on the trailer and a couple of the station workers drove him to the croc park in Darwin. The footage from my near-death moment wasn't captured and therefore not included in the episode because the cameras ended up in the mud. But the editors pieced together the rest of the day's adventure perfectly around it, making everything flow nicely, so at least our story wasn't ruined.

We started with that particular croc at 6 a.m. and it was 10 a.m. by the time we got him out and onto the trailer. I flew up high to get service again and touch base with Mick. The first text message that beeped through was *Come ASAP he's back in.*

Usually I'm hanging out for that kind of news, but I was so tired from all the travel that I couldn't think of anything worse than going *back* to Mount Bundy, but we didn't have a choice. This time I left the chopper at Moroak because Mick said he had a spare one not being used for the next couple of days. Jono, Willow, the camera crew and I drove together for the six-hour journey. We covered some serious ground and arrived at the trap in the late arvo, exhausted.

Tommy Nichols had left me some tranquilising needles before he had to return to Darwin, so I had them at hand for when we got the animal out. Thank god the croc was an easy one to move and get on the back of Mick's trailer. The croc was around 16 feet, a very similar size to the one at Moroak.

Mick was still in denial. 'There has to be another one, Matty, it can't be that croc. I don't think we need to move him out because he's not our guy.'

'Mate, he's already on the trailer and I can guarantee you it's the croc,' I assured him. 'That is one tiny waterhole so there are definitely no other big males in there. You are looking at the big monster you've been talking about.'

'You really think?' he asked, finally getting close to admitting defeat.

'Yes, mate, but the good thing is he won't be eating your cattle anymore.'

I felt bad because he was a little deflated that it wasn't the croc he thought it would be, especially because he'd been following it and tracking it for three years, telling me story after story about this monster. All his expectations were crushed in a heartbeat.

He took the croc to the Darwin croc park and the rest of us decided to suck it up and drive back to Moroak at 6 p.m. so we were ready for action first thing the next day. We didn't get in until 1 a.m. We fell into our swags, completely rooted.

The next morning, I called everyone around the fire. 'Okay, guys, we've caught one at Moroak, one at Adelaide River and we still have four cage traps and one panel trap here to rebait. Let's see if we can get a couple of the other bigger problem crocs. Once we're done here we'll go back to Adelaide River to finish off the story with Mick but no more to and froing, we'll go broke,' I said, alluding to the fact that, by this point, the show's travel expenses had spun out of control.

We gave ourselves another week at Moroak and popped to the neighbouring property, Flying Fox Station, in our downtime to help my mate Sully catch a couple of problem crocs on his property. It was reasonably easy work. The camera guys didn't even bother with filming any of it and came and had some fun with us. We got a lot done there and got back to our camp set-up at night for beers and a feed.

On the second last day at Moroak we caught a little croc next to the homestead. Even though it was small it was a good one to catch, given its proximity to the kids' play area. And it was a great opportunity to educate the kids about crocs. At only 10 or so feet long, he wasn't a major threat but we made sure we moved him a fair way up the river. There was a chance he might return, but it was a short-term deterrence and was better than doing nothing.

'All right, lads, you get trucking back to Darwin, I think we're done here. Jono and I will stay one more night to pack up, sling the traps out and stop in at Adelaide River to see if there's anything else Mick needs.'

About an hour after the guys took off, Jono and I flew over the panel traps to start hooking them on and slinging them out. We couldn't believe our eyes as we flew over one of the larger traps.

'No way, that can't be. There's the other big fella!' I said to Jono.

We'd been at Moroak for an entire week and it was so typical that on the last day we caught the one we'd been after. It was such a major part of the story because we'd been out there on the hunt for him for ages, but the obvious problem was that everyone had left.

'Just message Ash and he'll get it when he's at the next town. They don't really have much of a choice, they have to come back,' Jono said.

I flew up higher for reception and flicked the text over to Ash. I got a response from him once they'd reached Mataranka. *Ok, back we come. See you in the morning.*

Jono and I slept at the homestead because we'd already packed up the camp area. We were up at 6 a.m. and used the homestead wi-fi to confirm that the crew were on the road, heading for us. Then we flew straight over to the trap to get everything ready. There was a big mob of water, so I couldn't really see him.

'This guy is a bit camera shy,' I said to Jono. I poked around the trap until I noticed that an area of mesh had been warped. And then, just beneath the water's surface, was the bunged-up railing . . . and a big hole.

'No way, it can't be, this is just mean. What is the universe doing to us, Jonsy?! The bloody croc isn't here anymore!' I said.

Jono half-laughed and half-looked like he was going to cry with frustration.

And when the crew arrived, their reaction was much the same as Jono's.

'I'm so sorry, guys. Just hop right back in the utes, drive to Darwin, book in at the casino, my shout, and have cocktails by the pool. We all need a break,' I said, as the boys wandered back to the cars.

The post-production team did an awesome job at editing all of the behind-the-scenes headaches out of the two episodes. You wouldn't even know we had those problems or that I nearly got eaten. My planned contribution of factual information was also very limited in those two shows in the end, probably because I was so mentally exhausted from the running around. Nevertheless, we got the job done at both stations and I plan on going back to Moroak to get the one that got away. But, from all reports from Simon, there haven't been any more issues since we left, which is great to hear.

12
My wife

10.11.2017

My dearest Kaia,
Everyone likes to dream . . . me more than most. Kaia, having met you has exceeded any dreams I've ever had of meeting the best possible girl – I never imagined that I would be so lucky.

When it comes to explaining why this is so . . . to be honest, I don't even really know where to start because there are so many things that I love about you.

From the very onset, your zest for life, your passion for living and your desire to always learn captured my heart. The appreciation for some of the smallest things won over my admiration. You taught me that being rich on life experiences are what counts, not what's in the back pocket.

Since you have come into my life, I've learnt to see the positive in things, with your influence and optimistic outlook on life. Your selflessness and the time that you give so willingly to help others blows me away. Your kindness and generosity are just the start of your exceptional qualities that I have fallen in love with.

Every day, week and year, there is more and more that I see in you. The life that we live is one that is full of adventure, fun, excitement, love and travel, and the only thing that I would ever wish for is more time. This lifetime will never be enough, for you and me.

Kiki, there are so many generic internet vows and promises that I could rip off and say to you, like I will love you forever, protect you forever, provide for you forever, but you already know all that shit.

What I do promise is that I will always write you letters, cook your dinner (every now and then), hang up all your pictures around the house and even hook that magic fridge up or at least get Jono to do that for you. I promise to keep doing all the small things that count and all the big things that keep the magic alive, so you know just how much you mean to me.

I love you, Kiki, now and forever.

My wedding vows say a lot about what my wife Kaia means to me, but how we met and the adventures we've had along the way are pretty good telling as well.

The day I met Kiki was an interesting day. I was flying from Darwin to Perth to talk some things through with Troy, my business partner, who I was a bit disgruntled with at the time. Suited and booted, I was ready for a day of long meetings and negotiations in the office. But when I landed in Perth I learnt that Troy was in fact over on Rottnest Island, so my mate flew me over in his chopper and dropped me off on the beach.

I was taken aback by the beauty of the place. It was magnificent – with the whitest, finest sand and crystal-clear blue water. Ten or so boats, including Troy's, were rafted up in a little cove with music playing and people partying. I hopped onto Troy's boat still in my boots, jeans and collared business shirt. People were probably thinking, *What the? Who is this random?*

Troy was with his mates, and on the boat next to him was a group of incredibly beautiful women. I had been living up in the Northern Territory working on cattle stations, spending most of my days out in the bush. I wasn't really up with the times and didn't get exposed to women much. I was a complete fish out of water, with my scruffy hair and cowboy boots, amongst the bronzed sheilas in bikinis and manicured lads all wearing boardies that were so short they looked more like boxers.

'Let's forget about business today and have a few drinks together. We'll sort through things tomorrow,' Troy said to me.

'That suits me fine, I don't think I've stopped for a break in about four months.'

I sat back for a bit and watched everyone having fun. It felt good taking a moment out to do nothing. After a couple of beers, I thought I better try to blend in a little, so I got my shorts out of my backpack. They were marked with white paint and had a big tear in them, but they were better than my RMs and business shirt.

Everyone was having a great time. I got chatting to a young lad on the boat next to Troy's and while we were talking, one bird in particular caught my eye because she was beaming. She was smiling and laughing, and I mean properly smiling where her whole face lit up. It made me want to speak with her. All of a sudden, she came up to me.

'Hi, I'm Kaia,' she said, with so much warmth.

I didn't know what to say, I was shocked that she'd taken an interest in me. Usually, women like her think someone like me is a grubby bogan and tell me to get stuffed, but she approached me!

No one knew who the hell I was, and they all seemed like a pretty tight group of people. I was just this random gate-crashing a party and here I was, talking to the most beautiful girl of them all – actually, the most beautiful girl I'd ever seen.

'Where have you come from?' she asked me.

'Just up in Darwin.'

'Oh cool, have you been to the rock before?'

'Yeah, a few times, but I don't drive through the red centre much these days,' I said.

'Huh, red centre? No, not Uluru! The rock as in Rottnest – that's what we call it!' she said to me, laughing.

'Ah shit, I stuffed that one up,' I said, a bit embarrassed.

She didn't seem fazed by how out of place I was and wanted to talk. It was so refreshing. It was such a new thing for me to sit down and have a normal conversation with a woman and get along really well. I couldn't remember the last time a conversation with a bird flowed so smoothly – she even made me laugh, especially when her beer foamed up and spurted all over her face. We chatted the night away.

'What's got into you?' Troy said, making fun of me. 'Time to head back to my joint in Mandurah.'

'Nah, mate, I think I'll hang on the boat here and head back to Perth.'

Troy shook his head and laughed. 'Righto, see ya in the morning then!'

We wave-jumped all the way to Perth on the boat, trying to catch air each time we hit a wave, laughing our heads off. When Kaia leaned in and kissed me, I felt like a kid in a candy store.

I've had my fair share of nightmare relationships, and I was in and out of a pretty tumultuous one at the time. I wasn't happy, and I knew I had to end it for good, but I also wasn't looking for anyone else. I was over relationships and wanted to focus on work and my career. But out of nowhere this beautiful person popped up. There were a couple of other girls that day showing interest in me and a lot of the blokes trying to have a crack at Kaia, so we weren't a very liked couple. But we didn't give a shit about anyone else, we were in our own little world.

The next morning I asked Kaia for her number and she tapped it into my phone.

'Put yours in mine,' she instructed, and handed her mobile over.

I typed in the digits and gave it back. 'You okay?' I asked.

She looked really embarrassed. 'Um, sorry, this is really embarrassing, but what's your name again?'

I laughed. I never remember names but I remembered 'Kaia' of all names, and she couldn't remember something as simple as 'Matt'.

'I'm so sorry, I'm not usually like that, I just had a mental blank,' she said.

I could tell she was mortified, so I didn't make a thing of it. 'All good, Kaia.'

Troy picked me up, and he and I spent a couple of days in the office getting on top of things, but I couldn't get Kaia off my mind.

I had one night left in WA, so I called her and asked her to dinner. 'I'm in Mandurah at the moment,' I told her. 'How far is that from you?'

She laughed. 'You're over 70 km away from me and it's already 5 p.m. Maybe next time we'll catch up.'

'Yeah, righto, no worries. We'll keep in touch then,' I said, disappointed.

Troy had to stay in Mandurah and needed his car so I didn't have a way to get to her.

'You can catch the train,' Troy said to me after I hung up.

I was stoked to hear that I'd be able to get there. 'Oh yeah, I might just do that.'

Troy thought the whole situation was hilarious. 'Jesus, you're actually going to catch the train? I was only joking, but okay.'

I called Kaia back to tell her I was planning on taking the train and asked her what stop to get off at and if she'd pick me up in an hour's time. She also thought it was hilarious, but said she'd meet me. I was rapt.

I jumped off the train at Canning Highway in South Perth and her car was there waiting for me. I was happy to see that she actually showed up and didn't bail out, because she didn't really know me after all. We had pizzas at a joint near her place, which I noticed was very small, and we sat in a private booth at the back of the restaurant, away from anyone who might spot her. I was sure she was trying to hide me to start with. Nevertheless, we had another cracking night together and I went back to Darwin with a full heart.

We kept in contact over the next couple of months. Nothing full-on, though, because I was working through the aftermath of ending my last relationship and I wanted time to breathe. We met right at the start of egg-collecting season in 2014, which was actually perfect because I was out bush a lot and had time for my own thoughts.

One day I was in a buffalo wallow, trying to get some epic wildlife images and my phone fell out of my pocket and into the mud. At the same moment, a female croc came in on me and had a crack. I had to fend her off and, in the process, ended up completely covered in mud, with no crate, no stick and after rummaging around in the mud the phone wasn't to be found anywhere. I was in no rush to get back to town to get a new phone; I relished in the idea of being uncontactable.

A little while later, after I got back to town, I got my shit together, bought a phone and called Kaia.

'Hiya! How are you going?!' she cheered down the phone.

'Sorry I haven't been in touch,' I said. 'I lost my phone.'

She laughed lightheartedly, as if to say, *Yeah right, I'm not stupid.*

'No, I really did lose it,' I went on. 'You see, it fell out of my pocket in a buffalo wallow, while I was out collecting croc eggs. I stopped to take a photo, then a female croc came in to humbug me while I was on the nest, so I couldn't get it back.'

She laughed even harder. 'Wow, you're a really good liar!' she said.

Even though it was true, I realised how ridiculous the excuse sounded. I also knew that trying to convince her it was true was not going to work either. The thing is, she didn't seem all that fazed that we hadn't spoken in so long, so we just caught up and chatted like no time had passed. From then on, we spoke on the phone and texted every day and sent each other video messages too. We've got all the videos saved to a hard drive now, and Kaia dies with humiliation if I try to rewatch the ones of her.

During that time I made lots of trips to Perth, Margaret River and back to Rottnest, where I met up with Kaia. We hung out and got to know each other. On some of those trips I was so exhausted from working up north that I would sleep for two days straight before I could even function. But

Kaia's energy was so calming I felt recharged after being around her.

On a trip to Melbourne together, she told me she had landed a job in London and was planning on moving over in a few months' time. I knew that if she left I wouldn't see her again, so a couple of weeks later when we were chatting on the phone I just came out and asked, 'Hey, why don't you move in with me in Darwin instead of going to London?' We'd only been seeing each other for a few months, so it was a big call and I had no idea what she was going to say.

'Yeah, why not? If it doesn't work out it'll be a good story!' she replied.

I knew that it would work, though, because I knew I'd finally met the love of my life.

•

One of the best things about my wife is her love of adventure. She's not afraid to roll up her sleeves, hook in and get grubby, and she puts up with all of my antics. There are too many stories to share where I've got her to push her boundaries. She happily stands guard on a croc nest while I collect eggs, catches pigs when I need tucker for Tripod, hops on the back of crocs when I'm after an extra set of hands, keeps me company on long musters and puts up with my pet animals. There really isn't too much that bothers her.

When I first flew Kaia up to Darwin I wanted to put her through her paces and suss out if she was a princess. We'd been fishing for barra and flying around the waterfalls having some fun. Then the rain started to pour down and the swamps turned muddy.

'Okay, I'm going to land the chopper in a sec and I need you to jump on a pig. I've got to give my croc a feed today.'

She turned and looked at me with a half-smile on her face, like she wasn't sure if what I'd said was for real.

'Okay, go!' I yelled, once I'd landed the chopper.

Without hesitating she undid her seatbelt and jumped out, falling face first into the mud. She completely and totally ate shit. She stumbled up onto her feet, leaving her thongs behind, and sprinted towards the pack of pigs. Grabbing hold of a small one, she turned back to me, losing it laughing. How she caught it in the mud I don't know. The rain was thrashing down around her.

'What do I do?! What do you want me to do?!' she was screaming at me.

I swiped my hand across my neck in an 'abort mission' movement, signalling her to let the pig go. She got the gist and let it run off. After fishing her thongs from the mud, she jumped back in the chopper with me.

'I'm confused, don't you need a pig?' she asked.

'Nah, I saw you were wearing thongs and knew you'd eat shit in the mud. To be honest, I just wanted to have a laugh.'

'Oh my god, that's so mean!' She was not impressed, but I was.

When we bought our first house together in 2016 in a rural area 20 minutes from Darwin, Kaia set about decorating it into a beautiful home. She spent a week sugar-soaping, vacuuming, mopping and rearranging all our new furniture. We had a barney about the colour of our new couch and dining room chairs because Kaia wanted cream and I told her that it was a dumb idea in the bush, and that they'd be filthy in no time. She didn't listen and went on creating a display home in the Aussie outback, which I thought was a little silly, but I let her do her thing knowing it was only a matter of time before the cream turned crappy.

I guess I didn't help the cause, turning our house into a zoo within the first couple of weeks we were living there.

'Hun, come look here! I've got three dingo pups!' I called out to Kaia from downstairs one morning. I was so excited. 'We've got Albie, Ernie and Laya. Their mum must have been shot. We'll raise them here for a bit until they're old enough to let out near the shack where I found them.' Kaia didn't seemed fussed at the time, but now I know she actually wasn't keen on the idea at all! She just didn't want to say anything because we were still pretty early on in the relationship and she could tell I had my heart set on the dingoes.

I was busy working at the campsite and was coming and going from our new home, so Kaia had to keep an eye on the puppies as well as our two hounds, Naish and Apollo.

Two days later, I was driving back to our place and I saw a dead wallaby on the side of the Stuart Highway. I pulled over to inspect its pouch and discovered a tiny joey. I stopped off and got some wallaroo powder from the vet to feed the wallaby and took her home to Kaia in a little pouch bag.

'Here ya go, hun. You don't mind taking her around with you, do ya?'

'I don't think I've got much of a choice, do I?' she replied, but she was smiling.

'She'll be right,' I said, and Kaia looked at me funny.

'What?' I asked.

'That should be her name,' Kaia said. '*Shelby Wright* as in your favourite saying, *she'll be right.*'

With a name like that we had to keep her – and we had ourselves another new pet. I was stoked, but I could tell Kaia wasn't as wrapped with the idea. That same night I got a call from one of my employees asking me if I could take on a big cage with a heap of snakes in it, as the owner was moving interstate and had to get rid of them quickly. He explained that there were a couple of grass snakes, olive pythons and two epic albino pythons, which is what got me really excited.

'Yeah, righto, why not.'

I broke the news to Kaia. We agreed that I was only allowed to have them if the cage went in my office. But she wasn't so agreeable when I left on a tourism trip the next day and she had to look after seven snakes, two dogs, three baby dingoes, a wallaby and the six resident green tree frogs that had taken over our bathroom. She was defrosting mice for the snakes to eat, toileting the wallaby every three hours throughout the night (this is where you get up and prompt the animal to wee by rubbing their private parts with a wet wipe), and running the dingoes around while they clawed and nipped at her. Not to mention that Kaia had her own work as a communications manager to uphold. I'm sure at that point she was thinking a nice corporate banker in London might have been a much better option as a partner.

I got home from the trip and was cleaning the helicopter when I heard a scratching noise at the bottom of an old empty water tank on our property. I climbed up the ladder and looked in to see a beaten-up possum trapped at the bottom. I scaled down the wonky interior ladder and cupped it in my hat. It was malnourished and needed our help.

'Man, Kaia is going to kill me,' I said to myself. I walked through the front door and Kaia looked straight at my hat.

'What the fuck is that?' She was not impressed.

'Look, I know you've got a lot on your hands with work and the new animals, but this little girl was going to die if I didn't get her out of the water tank. I didn't have any choice. I had to bring her home.'

Kaia put her head in her hands and laughed. I don't think she knew what else to do.

That night, she went out for a drink with her girlfriends and left me to look after my menagerie of animals. I had a hell of a time. I let the two olive pythons out of the cage in my office and into our bedroom so they could roam around for a bit, and I did the same thing with the two albinos in the spare room. I had the possum slung across my chest in a pouch-like bag and the wallaby in another, feeding them together. Then I decided to let the dingo pups inside, just for a quick play and a bit of interaction with Naish and Apollo.

All five dogs ran riot. Ernie was jumping over Apollo on the couch, Laya got into the cushions, Albie knocked over the bin and was tearing its contents apart, Naish wanted to rip into the possum while poor Shelby Wright was wriggling around in the bag like no one's business. All I could think was, *Kaia is going to die when she sees the couch*. It had red and brown paw prints everywhere.

I fed the animals quickly, cleaned where I could, hung up the possum and Shelby in their pouches high on the hatch on our window louvres and lay back on the couch ready for Kaia to come home.

She arrived with some news. 'I made some calls tonight and found a home for Shelby, the possum and three dingoes,' she said, sitting on the couch with me. 'And even better news – everyone's coming to get them tomorrow morning!'

She was stoked, and I didn't blame her. The rest of the animals required full-time care and attention, so they were better off going to someone else who could offer that. And as long as I could keep my snakes, I was happy.

We went to bed early that night but at 2 a.m. I woke up to a piercing scream: 'MATT!!!'

I jumped up and turned the light on, and there was Kaia starfished on the bed with the big olive python wrapped around her left leg. She leapt up and started hopping around the place naked, trying to unravel it. If you were a fly on the wall you would have been in fits of laughter. I scurried around looking for the second snake and found it in the undies drawer.

'What THE HELL were you thinking, Matt?!' Kaia yelled, once the snakes were safely locked back in my office. 'Never ever do that again, that was mortifying!'

It was so fricken funny, but I did kind of feel bad because it would have come as a big fright for her.

Time and time again Kaia has proved her resilience, and tolerance for me and my shenanigans. She's well and truly gone through the ropes with me. She's my girl for good reason, and I wouldn't want to go through life with anyone else. Getting engaged and then married is my proudest achievement so far, and now I can't wait to have a family of little rascals together . . . but I hope they're more like her than me.

13
A bloke's dream

'You must get an unlimited supply of beer', 'You're a lucky bastard' and 'You're living a bloke's dream' is what most people say about my partnership with Great Northern Brewing Co. Sure, I enjoy drinking and promoting the beer, but what I like most is that the brand is built around things I value – friendship, adventure and fun. Back in 2016, Great Northern was an up-and-coming beer. It was popular in northern Australia, and was building its presence elsewhere. Lots of people around Darwin drank it, including me, and people used to say to me, 'You drink enough of that stuff, Matty, you should do something with them one day.'

Then 'one day' happened and my manager, Nick, called me.

'Mate, I've been chatting with CUB [Carlton & United Breweries] and they're keen to get you on as the brand ambassador for Great Northern. I think it's a good fit, what do you reckon?' he asked.

'Sounds good to me. Actually, it sounds great,' I replied.

Great Northern came up with *True North*, a miniseries of ads shared as short films featuring Willow, Jono and me. Exploits and escapades are second nature to us, so the miniseries was essentially us doing what we do best – running amok and enjoying beers together. The funny part was that each ad came with a detailed script and storyline, but when it came time to filming, we didn't follow any of it. We were in our natural element so our banter, misadventures and one-liners happened organically, without the need to stage anything. The final product ended up being a miniseries that was mostly unscripted and shot documentary-style. In that way, the ads feel real, and I think people can tell there is an authenticity to them. That's why the ads and the campaign have been so successful.

•

Our first gig working with Great Northern took us to Cairns to go marlin fishing, hiking and diving. Each adventure formed one of three ads for *True North*, part one. I'd never been marlin fishing, before but I'd heard and seen a lot about it and was itching to get on the water.

I flew Naish, my dog and best mate of 12 years, over for the adventure too. She passed away unexpectedly from kidney failure at the beginning of 2018, so the trip ended up being my last big getaway with her and holds very special memories. Naish followed me around for that whole day of fishing, sitting in my shadow, licking my face and standing at the front of the boat, smiling into the wind. I remember looking at her and thinking how happy she was.

The weather itself was rough as guts. It was coming into the wet so the weather wasn't very forgiving, and the fish weren't biting which was a bit of a problem, given that the script was pretty much: *Boys go fishing, catch a big marlin, cook up dinner and enjoy beers as the sun sets*. None of these things were happening or even looked like they were going to happen. Instead, Willow got revoltingly seasick and we only caught three small fish. But it didn't end up mattering because a sub-story effortlessly developed. As the day went on the lack of fish evolved into a light-hearted competition between the three of us.

'Whoever catches the first fish in these conditions really is the best fisherman, because it's near on impossible,' Willow declared.

So it was game on, and the jokes and set-ups between us all kept coming, and Naish turned into the fourth star of the show with her big presence and personality. It ended up being a cracking day on the water and an epic first ad for the *True North* series.

The other good thing with Great Northern is that everyone I've worked with really believes in the brand, loves the outdoors lifestyle, thrives on adventure and thinks outside of the box. I haven't come across anyone who works for Great Northern, or CUB for that matter, who is caught in a rigid corporate mindset. They are all open to new ideas and new ways of doing things.

The Great Northern marketing team, along with our producer, drafted another great script for the second ad of the first series, which involved a hike through a rainforest to a waterfall. We saw pictures and videos of the waterfall before we left; it was spectacular, and we loved the sound of the planned activities and storyline, which was *Guys hike through the rainforest, up to a waterfall, have a swim, then finish with beers and camping out.*

Dan Walkington, who is the producer and main editor of *Outback Wrangler*, was the contracted producer for the *True North* series. Dan is a legend of a bloke and is responsible for editing all of my TV content, so he knows what he's doing. However, on this particular shoot, he was a little misinformed on the logistical side of things. Us lads were from Darwin and Dan is from Sydney so none of us knew the lay of the land around Cairns and Dan got his information about the waterfall's whereabouts over the phone, not on the ground. He called ahead to speak to the local tour guides and accommodation owners we were engaging and got the down-low, but in hindsight he probably should have done a recce himself. But Dan seemed confident, so we packed our swags, camping gear and a big esky full of beers and headed off down the path towards the waterfall.

'So, Dan the man, how long's this walk?' I asked.

'Not far, Matty,' he said. 'The guy I spoke to said it's close by, so I'm figuring it will be about 15 or so minutes until we get there.'

We wound through the rainforest along a narrow path. Everyone was taken aback by the beauty, commenting on the trees and wildlife. Then the path began to steepen, and by 'steepen' I mean it became almost vertical.

'Have we gone the right way, Dan? I don't imagine we'd be walking up that,' Willow asked, pointing to the mini-Mount Everest in front of us.

'Sorry, lads, all the signs say it's this way. I must have misjudged the distance a bit,' Dan said.

I had thought we were walking a couple of ks to a relaxing swimming hole when in fact we were only half-way through a five-kilometre trek up a mountain with a 30-kilogram esky, backpacks and camping gear. Our camera man, Jez, stopped filming momentarily as things turned a little tense. None of us were angry, we were just completely exhausted as we walked and walked, passing the esky from person to person every hundred metres. The path flattened out briefly as it connected with a bitumen road with a sign that said we were one kilometre away from the main waterfall.

'Gee, still another kilometre. I don't know if my legs have it in them,' I said.

Dan was up ahead and waved over a four-wheel drive coming down the incline. He exchanged words with the driver then came jogging towards us with a big smile.

'I offered the bloke fifty bucks to drive us up the rest of the hill! Come on, jump in!' He was so chuffed with his little advance.

'Dan, you do know, though, this lift is an hour-and-a-half and 10 blisters too late?' I joked.

'I know, Matty, I'm sorry about that,' he replied.

'All good, these things happen, mate. It's probably a good thing we're burning off the beer we're about to drink!' I said, lightheartedly.

We made it to the waterfall, which was beautiful and made the hike worthwhile. Once we were up there it was bliss. It was a Monday afternoon and out of the peak holiday season, so no one else was there. Always the most adventurous of us all, Jono scaled up the rocks the moment we arrived, jumping off into the pool with a double backflip. I followed him but chickened out mid-move and mid-air, and hit the water with an awkward bellyflop. And Willow, well, Willow didn't even fancy going in. We were the three musketeers with different levels of musketeering when it came to waterfalls. Willow kept the beers cold and the fire going and started cooking the steaks. We had an awesome feed around the campfire before calling it a night.

The next morning, we jumped into two hired four-wheel drives. Dan had reviewed the previous day's hiking footage and decided we all looked drained, so he wanted us to recreate our arrival at the waterfall, making out in the advert that we'd driven there.

'Re-enacting like this never goes well,' I grumbled to Jono as we climbed into the car.

Dan overheard. 'Yeah, I agree. I'm not a fan either, but we don't have much of a choice for this one, unfortunately.'

So we hit the road and soon found a river crossing with a bit of shallow water and a sandy bank.

'Okay, Matty, can you please go through that bit of water there and make out like you're four-wheel driving?' Dan asked.

'Sure can,' I said. I was a bit gung-ho behind the wheel, and accelerated too hard, nosediving the car straight into the water. The wheels lost traction with the ground and we began to float down the river.

'Oh, big problem,' I remarked.

Willow and Jono thought it was hilarious because I had insisted on taking the wheel and then had completely messed things up while the cameras were rolling. I was really stuffing up Dan's retake.

We eventually got traction again and inched out onto the bank. Then we jumped into the other car so we could try a second take while the crew sorted out the bogged vehicle. We found a shallower spot in the river to cross and Willow climbed onto the back of the car with a GoPro, to capture everything from another vantage point. But I hit a little ditch as we were crossing, which threw Willow off balance and he fell off the back and straight into the creek, saturating himself. He jumped back in and we eventually got across and booted up to the waterfall.

Dan was stoked, the misadventures had woven perfectly into the story, and so we called it a day. We finished the trip off the next morning with a diving voyage out on the ocean, which was fun but very cold. Jono's suggestion of rounding off the day with impromptu beer-battered fish on the barbie with a Great Northern made the perfect end to our Cairns trip.

•

At the end of 2017, Jono, Willow and I went to Port Douglas for round two of *True North* filming. Kaia works in communications, and at the time, she and I were flat out in the middle of writing this very book, so I felt a little bad leaving her in the office and heading off to Port Douglas.

'Honey, next week I'll be away again for a week working,' I said to her. 'You have enough recorded content to continue writing, don't you?'

'Yeah, I've got a heap,' she replied. 'What do you have on?'

'Ah . . . just something for Great Northern,' I said.

'Oh yeah, a corporate talk?' she asked.

'Ah, not quite,' I said. 'We've got another *True North* series to film.'

She looked at me with a big grin. 'Ohhhh, *that* sort of work.'

'Haha, yep, I'm afraid so! This time it's horseriding, fishing and whitewater rafting, so should be sick!' I said, bouncing around with excitement.

'Yes, I'm sure it will be, hun. Well, you enjoy that "work" of yours and I'll see you tonight to hear more about your plans,' she said, kissing me.

'They say if you love what you do, you never have to work a day in your life!' I said cheekily.

•

The A-team was back together with the Great Northern marketing crew, our cameraman Jez, soundy Row, and Dan. By this point, Naish's health was deteriorating, so I brought my younger dog Apollo along for his first proper adventure. This time around, we all got to choose our activity ahead of the shoot and work with Dan to flesh out a storyline to go with it. Willow chose fishing, Jono chose horseriding and I chose whitewater rafting.

After an early first night we woke up at dawn and drove out to the Daintree River, ready for Willow's fishing adventure. We launched the boat at the ramp and while Willow was giving us an overview of the day's plans, I got distracted by some movements in the mangroves. I sprinted to the water's edge and jumped on a three-foot croc.

'You're a goose!' Jono called out to me.

I was thrilled with the little fella and brought it back over to show the crew. Everyone had a hold of it and we talked crocs for a bit.

'Come on now, Matty, we're filming a fishing adventure not a croc-catching mission. We're not in Darwin anymore, put the croc back and let's get going!' Willow said. He wasn't pleased with me hijacking his activity, but I couldn't help myself. And it was worthwhile because the croc catch actually did end up making the final cut.

Once we were out on the river we discovered fishing was hard going because there was very little movement in the water, and we gave Willow a bit of slack for it. We get pretty spoilt with fishing up in the Territory, so an afternoon consisting of only a few bites and a couple of trevally felt very quiet. After stitching Willow up by putting a dead fish on the end of his line, blowing a boat engine and trying to paddle back to shore with an esky lid (we ended up getting towed by the film crew's boat) we arrived at our camping spot. The rest of the support crew met us there and fixed our boat, and then we took it for another quick adventure.

At sunset, we came across some pythons wrapped around a tree branch overhanging a narrow channel and stopped to do a bit more filming. However, this slice of the story didn't make it into the ads, thanks to a minor mishap between Jono and a tree branch.

Willow was steering the boat and we had Jez and Row on board, filming. We turned around in a tight area with lots of overhanging trees.

'Shit, watch out, watch out, duck!' I yelled to Jez and Row, who had their backs to us as they filmed at the front of the boat. They ducked and missed but Jono, who was standing just ahead of Jez and Row, turned right around to see what was going on and headbutted a low-lying branch.

'Ahhhh!' Jono yelled, and we stopped the boats.

He was holding his head, laughing at how silly he'd been.

Blood was pissing out everywhere. The guys kept filming for a bit, but then Dan called it quits.

'Let's wrap it up, fellas. I think this misadventure is too much of a miss than a hit. No one wants to see blood.'

We got back to camp and Dan pulled out his make-up kit, plugging up Jono's face with thick foundation. Jono was less than impressed by the whole ordeal, but we all thought it was pretty funny. If you watch the '3 Men in a Tinnie' ad, you'll see that at the start Jono looks nice and fresh, but once we get to the camping spot he has a noticeable cut on his head, which features in the rest of the ads we filmed on this shoot.

Before we went on Jono's horseriding adventure we spent a day getting things sorted for whitewater rafting. A mate of mine, Jim, owns a cane farm property up near Cairns, so I organised to go out to his place to source some bamboo and gear to build our rafts with. I hadn't been to Jim's Cairns place before, and he wasn't around to help us with directions, so it took a bit of guesswork to find the joint. We located the shed and helped ourselves to the saws hanging up. There was some fish netting and a few plastic drums lying around too, which we loaded into our trailer, then got hacking into the bamboo.

Dan was stoked with the whole set-up. 'This is ideal, Matty. There's everything we need here for the rafts!'

Mucking around and doing our thing, we sawed our way through a little patch of bamboo. Apollo was running rampant, chasing birds around the paddock, having a great time.

Then a ute pulled up.

'G'day, guys, what are you doing?' the old fella driving it asked.

'Hey, mate, we're friends of Jim's. We're just taking some timber off his block for some rafts we're making,' I told him.

'Yeah, okay. Well, I'm not sure who Jim is but this is actually my block you're on,' he told us.

'Oh, really?! I'm so sorry, man, I had no idea!' I said to him, shocked.

I felt terrible. There we were, on some random person's property, with three of his saws in our hands, standing in front of a pile of his cane we'd just cut down.

'Don't stress, Matty, all good. Love your show, by the way,' he said.

Phew, I thought. Boy, were we lucky that he knew who we were and was okay about the entire situation, because we could have been seriously stung for trespassing.

'My young fellas are fans. If you don't mind, can I bring them up here for a picture?' he asked.

'God, yeah, it's the least we can do, mate!' I said, feeling totally relieved and equally embarrassed.

The guy came back up with his kids, their cousins, their cousins' friends, his neighbours and his neighbours' neighbours. We said hello and got a few photos. They were lovely people and the bloke's two young fellas were keen to help.

'You can leave all the material here if you like and come back when you're ready to film,' they said. We took up the offer and said we'd come by again.

Day three was horseriding, which was a nostalgic choice by Jono, who reminisced about the rides he and I went on as kids. Apollo was great around the horses and followed closely on the ground, running up terrain and paddling through water. Willow decided he wanted to go on a motorbike, which worked well for all of us because he could cart the esky with him.

Jono and I bounced around the place and began to feel confident in the saddle.

'I'm really starting to get the hang of this,' Jono said to me as we picked up into a canter down one of the fire breaks.

'Yeah, I'm not feeling too rusty myself,' I said back.

We got into the rhythm and made our way through the rainforests and water channels. But Jono had spoken a little too soon. He fell off his horse twice along the way, into the water, eating humble pie.

After a beautiful day we arrived at our camping spot to see Willow with beers on ice and fresh mud crabs for dinner.

'You beauty! You've delivered the goods today,' I said.

We didn't have any injuries, breakdowns or things go terribly wrong. It was actually one of the most picturesque and peaceful days I've had, and it was finished off perfectly. We needed some rest, especially ahead of what I had planned for the next day.

I called the two young lads from the cane farm and let them know we were coming over to collect our rafting gear. We rocked up, and there they were with these big grins on their faces. They're standing there with these three perfectly made rafts ready for us to take.

'Wow, lads, these are insane!' Jono said.

Each raft was solidly constructed with plastic water drums, bamboo sticks, rope and netting pulling everything together. I didn't want to tell them that part of the storyline was us constructing the rafts, so I asked if they minded if we took some material to make a couple more as backups and invited them along for the fun.

'Well, there's three rafts here,' Willow said, 'and you and Jono are making one more each, so I may as well use one of these sick rafts to put it to the test.'

'Ah, cheating are we, Willow? You don't back your own raft-building abilities?' Jono joked.

'Nah, nah, not at all, I'm just interested to see how it goes.'

'Okay then, mate, you take one of them and I bet I'll still pip ya!' I said, stirring up a bit of a challenge between us.

We arrived at the rapids and they didn't look like a simple walk in the park.

'Wow, Matty, you've really thrown us in the deep end here,' Willow remarked. 'You've always got to take it to that next level, don't you? That turbulence is definitely no joke.' He was right. The rapids were raging, and had some good power behind them.

'All for one and one for all, hey!' I said, as we walked to the top of the rapids. The young fellas were mucking about with their own rafts, taking it all in, as happy as can be.

The race was on to see who could reach the full Great Northern esky first, located about a kilometre downstream. I thought I was going to win, Jono was also pretty confident about his rafting abilities and I'd successfully made Willow doubt himself, as he'd revised his own prediction by saying he would be happy just to make it down in one piece. We bounced into the water, but as we got going I turned around to see Apollo jump off the rocks, following me in.

'Oh no!' I started paddling backwards as I watched him get caught in a whirlpool, going around and around in circles. I kept paddling back until I reached him, and then pulled him out and into the arms of one of the young fellas. I looked down the rapid and saw Willow fly in front of Jono, taking the lead. Jono moved closely behind, riding his raft like a rodeo bull. Once the guys noticed what had happened they jumped out and legged it back up to the top so we could do a rerun but, sadly for me, Willow took the win again fair and square, followed by Jono, and I came in deadset last. But the adventures weren't over yet.

'I'm in big trouble, guys!' Willow called as he got out of the water, rummaging around the rocks in the shallow water.

'Why, what happened?' I asked.

'My wedding ring got caught and came off me finger.'

'UH OH! BIG trouble, my man, you've got no hope finding it in these rapids,' I told him.

'I got my phone number engraved on the inside in case I ever lost it. I just didn't plan on losing it somewhere like this.' He looked around, worried.

'Wait, did you just say your ring is engraved with your number?!' Jono and I said at the same time, laughing.

'That's the weirdest thing I've ever heard,' Jono continued.

'Yeah, how does a phone number even fit on a ring?' I added.

'Shut up you two,' Willow said. He sighed. 'I'll wait and tell the missus when I get home.'

'Good thinking, mate,' Jono said.

Our trip ended the next day and we headed home, talking about all the good times from filming.

'I hope we can do a *True South* next time and head down the coast somewhere to do another series. They're the best fun,' Willow said.

'Ditto. They're bloody good, mate,' I agreed.

•

At the start of 2018, Willow was around at my joint having a barbie and, strangely enough, we were talking about our trips to Cairns, reminiscing about the fun, when Willow's phone rang.

'Get out of here, there's no way,' he exclaimed, after answering it.

'What is it?' I asked once he'd hung up.

He turned to me. 'A bloke found my ring!'

'You're joking?!' I said.

'For real, he's posting it up to me tomorrow. He reckons

he found it in a side pool, stuck in a crevice. Then he saw my number on the inside. It wasn't a bad idea doing that after all, was it?!' Willow said.

'I just can't believe your luck, mate, that's incredible!'

14

Caught off guard

It was a nice cool night in the middle of the dry season, and Jono and I were camping out in my caravan on La Belle Station, located approximately 180 km southwest of Darwin. I had bought the 1970s caravan off Gumtree a week earlier for 400 bucks. It resembled an empty tin can and was falling apart in most places. It was short on a toilet but had a working stove and provided good enough shelter for Jono and me. We needed a base during a week-long croc-catching mission on the cattle station, and with the cool nights I thought a caravan would provide better shelter than mozzie dome tents.

I'm usually a pretty heavy sleeper, but I woke up in the middle of the night with a full bladder. I was so comfy wrapped up in my sleeping bag with the crisp air blowing through the open windows chilling my face, that I prolonged my pee for a good hour until my bladder felt like it was going to burst. Reluctantly, I got up in my jocks, still half-asleep, and stumbled out the door, walking straight into something.

'Shit!' I blurted out.

Our tarpaulin awning had partly fallen down and had swiped me across the face, bringing me to my senses. I tied the blue tarp back to the pole and closed the botchy door behind me, then turned to look out over the lagoon. We'd parked the caravan about 100 metres from the water in a really pretty spot, with the big silver moon splashing its reflection down over the water's surface. The night owls hooted in the trees and I could hear other birds chirping too: the moon was giving off such a strong glow, they must have thought it was daytime. The frogs were also making one hell of a racket, and I was surprised the chorus of animals hadn't woken me earlier.

La Belle shares an eastern boundary with Litchfield National Park and, in some places, the property is just as picturesque as the Park. Most of the land is made up of marine floodplains full of wildlife and covered in native wetland grasses, with lots of crocodiles and heaps of big ones at that. The property is divided into 34 paddocks and can hold about 30,000 head of cattle. Cattle and crocs don't mix well, so the station owner had asked Jono and me to do a big relocation of about 30 crocs. It was perfect timing because the local crocodile park needed a top-up of breeding stock. The station owner also told us to keep an eye out for a massive croc that had been giving him grief, intimidating the station workers while they were fishing.

I'd heard the mustering pilots talking about this croc over the years; it had become a bit of a legend. People said it was around 18 feet, and it had a reputation for being able to carry an entire cow in its jaws across the floodplains. You usually see big crocs with a leg or head but never a full cow because of the sheer weight. So this croc had to be one hell of a monster animal. Jono and I knew he was hanging around because we'd seen him on our motion-sensor cameras, but we hadn't sighted him in the flesh yet.

The air outside felt like it was getting cooler by the second and I didn't want to stand still for long. I walked over to a bunch of trees nearby, where our semitrailer was parked, and relieved my bladder. Down that way were four crocs tied to the bases of tree trunks with a pen around the outside of them, on long ropes so they could still move around a bit.

We had slung these crocs out of a turkey nest, which is kind of like an above-ground dam with built up sides. I used a chopper to get the job done the day before, and we were keeping the crocs in the cool until a truck came by to relocate them to the farm. The four medium-sized females in this pen were carefully taped up with hessian over their eyes to keep them calm. I could hear the thud of one croc's tail slapping the ground, and another one sliding around the pen. The smell of the rotten leftover bait in the semitrailer wafted towards me, so I quickly finished my business and went to head back to bed. I turned and kicked something hard.

'Ugh!' I put my foot down and then stuck it out again, this time more gently, to try to feel what was in my way. I squatted to get a closer look.

'Strike me dead!' I said, as the blood starting pumping through my body. Lying right there, stretched out on the ground in front of me, was an enormous thumping croc tail. There was no denying it – it was the monster croc. He must have come up to investigate the rotting pig bait and got caught out high and dry. I stood still for a moment, then suddenly the croc swiped its tail, clipping me and sending me arse-up into the dirt. It reared up into the air, seized one of the trailer tyres in its jaws and shook the shit out of it, nearly ripping it off. I scrambled to my feet and moved around to the other side of the trailer.

'Jonoooo!' I screamed, at the top of my lungs. 'Come here now!'

The croc moved a couple of metres back towards the water but stopped in its tracks, uncharacteristically.

Jono scampered out of the caravan in his jocks. Thank god he had heard me.

'Get the rope and harpoon!' I called out to him. He ran, scooped up the gear and bolted in my direction, eyes wide open. I ripped the rope out of his hands and sprinted for the croc with Jono close behind me. I wanted to get in front of it to put a head rope on his snout before he reached the water but I wasn't fast enough. The croc had started moving again, heading into the lagoon.

'Quick, get one into him, Jonsy!'

Jono speared the harpoon into the back of the croc's neck, hitting it bang-on. With the croc attached, the harpoon line started reeling further and further out with the croc attached, while Jono ran behind, keeping a strong hold of the reel at the other end. I went like the clappers, slipping and sliding in the mud, down to the bank where our tinnie was parked. 'Jump in, mate, and get another one ready!'

We needed reinforcement with a croc this big, one harpoon wouldn't cut it. Jono was already all over it, prepping the second harpoon in the boat.

The technique of harpooning is often misunderstood. When people hear the word 'harpoon' they automatically think negative thoughts because of the horrific practice used by Japanese whalers. Those harpooning techniques kill whales slowly and painfully, and the thought of it makes me sick with anger. The hunters often use a toggling harpoon, which involves the top half of a harpoon point detaching into the body of the whale; twisting horizontally into the flesh, lodging the head of the harpoon through its skin and blubber and underneath its muscle. Whales have a non-valvular structure of blood vessels, so when even the smallest of harpoons pierces their skin a deadly drain of blood gushes out and the animal bleeds out. It is nothing short of grotesque.

Crocodile harpooning, on the other hand, is a different kettle of fish. Firstly, the wellbeing of the animal is our primary concern and we harpoon to relocate, not to kill. Our technique follows the Australian government's *Code of practice for the humane treatment of wild and farmed Australian crocodiles*. It is a quick, efficient method for capturing crocs, which reduces the period of struggle time and therefore stress on the animal. All harpoons are designed and built to ensure that its barbs penetrate no deeper than below the crocodile's skin so that it doesn't damage muscle and other underlying body tissues. The barbs are never longer than 2.5–3 cm to prevent unnecessary penetration and we always try to place the harpoon in the neck area of a crocodile, which is the safest and most pain-free for the animal. It is also the most practical place because it helps bring the croc to the surface. If we were to hit the croc on the tail, the animal would have the upper hand: it would whip its tail around and be able to keep itself at the bottom of the water, so we would be attempting to catch it all day long.

We had no one to call for back-up and were in a tiny tinnie in the middle of a croc-infested lagoon, wearing nothing but our undies.

'We're not the most prepared are we, mate,' Jono said, grinning.

'We're pretty good at getting ourselves into situations like this and we're usually just as good at getting ourselves out of them, so let's hope the same applies tonight,' I replied.

'What do you mean "tonight"?! Mate, it's one-thirty in the MORNING and we're half-naked trying to catch the biggest croc in Australia!'

We both lost it laughing. So far, things were going well. The croc seemed pretty worn out; he still had the first harpoon attached to the rope in him and he wasn't putting up a fight. I continued to steer the boat, and Jono reeled in some of the loose line as we caught up to the croc in the water.

'All right, mate,' I said. 'Any minute now it's going to come up alongside the boat for a breath of fresh air. You need to get another harpoon in the same spot.'

'I can't see anything under that water,' Jono commented.

'Yeah, I know, that's why you've got to wait for that head to emerge. When it comes up for air, get another one of those harpoons into him.'

'Yep, yep, righty-o.' Jono took the headlamp and secured it to his head.

A big spray of water burst through the lagoon's surface as the croc rose, releasing a burst of air from his nostrils. Jono propelled another harpoon at him and clipped him in the back of the neck, right beside the other harpoon.

'Perfect shot, well done!' I shouted.

Away he darted, with a burst of power.

'This is ideal, we've got two in him,' I said, confidently.

'If we get him, I'll be very surprised if he's not the biggest croc ever caught in Australia,' Jono replied. 'It's the biggest I've ever seen in the wild, that's for sure.'

I agreed with Jono. This beast was more prehistoric dinosaur than modern crocodile.

'Now it's time for the head rope, then we'll work out how to get him out of here.'

By this time it was 2 a.m. We were tired and the insects were thicker than ever. With every breath I got another mouthful of mozzies, and their relentless biting was driving me mad.

'I can even feel these suckers biting at my balls,' Jono said.

So could I. They were biting through the material, having a crack at every inch of skin. I couldn't think straight.

'Pass me the lines and make yourself some clothes,' I said to Jono, nodding towards the hessian, gaffer tape and a small knife in the corner of the boat. He looked confused, and didn't move. Then the croc jerked the lines, so I turned the motor on to move along with him some more until he stopped again for a rest.

'Here, like this, I'll show you,' I said, switching the motor off and turning to Jono.

I cut some sheets of hessian and wrapped them around my calf, gaffer-taping them to hold them in place. I did my calves and quads on both legs, the full length of my arms and then mummified myself with the hessian around my torso, taping it tight. Jono looked impressed and followed suit.

Every time there was a bit of reprieve with the croc and we became stagnant in the water, I would turn the motor off and hold the lines while Jono taped up another part of his body. We looked like idiots, but it stopped us from getting cold and bitten.

We booted up the river again. I thought I could see something faint in the near distance so I cut the engine and let the croc pull us along. Sure enough there was a big log coming up in the water that I didn't see early enough. It was too late: we hit the log and Jono flipped off sideways into the pitch-black water. Luckily, he still had a hold of the rope. I grabbed the two reels wedged in the footwell to make sure they didn't fall overboard. Jono had one hand on the rope and was pulling himself in towards the boat, kicking frantically at the same time.

'Try to keep your splashing to a minimum!' I called out.

He stopped moving about and started doing breaststroke with his head above water. He swam up to the back end of the tinnie, panting crazily, with complete shock in his eyes.

'That spooked me out, that was close, mate,' he gasped, when he was safely back on board.

I knew it was too close, and I also knew we weren't at all equipped to catch the croc, but it was now or never with this guy.

'Jono,' I said, 'I promise we'll go back if we can just get a head rope on the croc first.'

Jono wasn't happy. 'Okay then.'

I turned to restart the motor and up came the croc behind me, attracted by the noise. He grabbed the boat's engine in his jaws and tore the whole thing out, leaving a gaping hole.

'We just lost our engine, Jono,' I said, with a touch of panic.

'Shit, now what?'

We both moved to the front of the tinnie to balance out the sinking end of the boat. But water started flowing into the back. We were right in the middle of the lagoon, with about 50 metres on either side of us until dry land.

'Grab those empty water bottles and foam balls,' I instructed Jono. 'We'll attach floats to the ends of the lines so we can locate the croc in the morning.'

We tied the croc off quick-smart, and hoped the floats would hold up until daybreak. There we were, Jono and me, sitting up the front of the tinnie trying to keep the back up and out of the water, paddling desperately with a couple of bottles. Each time I looked out across the water, I saw little crocodile eyes glistening like fairy lights; the water was covered in them. The big croc had left us alone, but there were hundreds of other crocs that wouldn't have minded having a crack. More and more water was pouring into the boat and then, about 10 metres from the bank, our tinnie did a *Titanic* and plummeted into the water. We launched ourselves forward and swam the last couple of metres to the bank.

'We made it!' Jono was relieved.

I looked around me. 'Well, not quite, mate. We're on the wrong side of the lagoon. Our camp is set up across the other side.'

'Ya fucking kidding me?'

'I wish I was.'

We made our way back up around the lagoon, moving around a few estuaries as we walked. The jungle was thick and totally dark in places, so going barefoot wasn't great. Sharp sticks stabbed into the arches of my feet and I walked with my hands in front of me, trying to feel my way. I just prayed and prayed that we didn't find ourselves coming head to head with a big bull or buffalo. After another hour and a half we staggered into the camp clearing. We had cuts and scratches, busted feet and busted brains. Without even rinsing off, we ripped off our hessian outfits and stumbled into our beds at 4.30 a.m.

My watch alarm went off at 7 a.m. and we jumped in the chopper to get an aerial view of the lagoon.

'Look, Jonsy,' I said, pointing. 'The two floats are still there! Let's hope the crocodile is too.'

We flew straight to the homestead and asked for a new boat and some manpower.

The station owner immediately agreed. 'We're not worried about the boat, just don't get yourself chewed on,' he said.

'Nah, we'll be right, hey, Jono?'

'Yep,' he replied bluntly. Jono was probably thinking, *Don't give Matty your bloody boat, you'll never see it again!* He was done with it all, I could tell.

'Will four fellas do?' the station owner asked.

'That will be perfect,' I said.

We got everything sorted: the guys would take the new boat down and bring a couple of utes in case we needed them.

There was no messing about. When the boat arrived, Jono and I put it in the water and headed for the floats. Two big marble-like brown eyes popped up to say hello as soon as we reached them.

I was stoked. 'We've still got him!'

Then out came his set of snapping jaws. Each tooth

stretched two-and-a-half inches out of his mouth, his head was almost two feet wide and about four feet long.

'No wonder he tore the back of the boat off,' I said to Jono. 'It would've been like a little toy for a croc this size.'

As I was talking, the croc pushed out of the water even more and Jono dropped the head rope around its top jaw, pulling it tight. He got him first go, once again.

'You're on fire, mate!' I yelled, delighted.

We slowly towed the croc through the water and close to the bank. We had to get him onto land before I could tape him up. He was too big to do it in the water, and if I tried I knew I would be dead meat.

'Righto, mate, jump out onto the bank and tie the croc to that tree,' I said to Jono. 'I'll run up to the caravan and get the boys to bring the utes closer. If we need to, we can probably use the chopper to pull him up a bit.'

The croc was still underwater when I arrived back with the boys. Jono was keeping tension on the rope, concentrating and staying calm.

'He's just at the end of the rope, about six feet under, but when he emerges he's going to come out with a lot of force so we have to be careful that when we pull him, his bottom jaw doesn't get stuck in the mud, okay?' I said to the fellas.

'Okay,' everyone answered.

We had the rope wrapped around the tree and tied to the car, set up like a pulley to manoeuvre the croc out of the water. All eyes were on the monster as it appeared unwillingly. With each acceleration and pull, he moved about a foot or so.

I could hear the station workers gasp as the croc showed its impressive size. But we were so focused on the animal that the guys in the ute didn't realise how much pressure they were putting on the rope around the tree.

'Argh!' I yelled, as the rope ripped backwards through my hands, burning them raw.

I turned around to hear an almighty crack and watched as the tree snapped in half. The rope went to pieces and the car catapulted forward. Jono fell over and I just stood there, dead still, in shock. In that split second the monster took the opportunity to belly down the bank like a snake into the water. It swam away frantically, with its tail whipping to and fro. I scrambled around trying to get a hold of what was left of the rope, but it was too late and the rope was too short.

That was it. The croc got away and there was no getting him back in the one day we had left. He escaped before we could properly measure him, so I never got to know how big he really was. I have gone back to try to catch him on six different occasions but have had no luck. I still to this day get texts and pictures from mustering pilots of the elusive croc carrying half-chewed cows in his mouth or of his kill that he's stashed in the jungle somewhere and left to rot. La Belle Station has changed hands in recent years, but the same croc is giving the same headaches to the new owners and it's still one of my missions to return and move him out. He was once a myth, but now we know he's the real deal and he's become a bit of a legend in the area.

15

Success

As a young lad, I seized every opportunity to have fun, and loved nothing more than being free. Toeing the line and being responsible wasn't something I ever thought or cared about. I just lived every day as it came, doing whatever I felt like, and went to bed each night planning the next day's mischief. School was a bore and I didn't like my teachers much. The more I got in trouble and punished, the better I became at not getting caught. Punishment is meant to deter bad behaviour, but that never worked for me.

Growing up, everyone would always say *Get good marks, perform in class and you'll succeed*. My question was always, *Yeah, but succeed in what?* As a troublesome teenager I had no idea what the future would hold. All I knew was that life was for living and every minute I was asleep was a minute lost. 'You can sleep when you're dead' is one of my favourite sayings. Wasting time has never been on my agenda. I have a tendency to swing too far over into the land of work and forget to stop and smell the roses, so where is the balance I asked myself. My goals as a young bloke were to:

- work hard
- be financially stable
- buy a house
- meet a life partner
- have kids to pass on everything I know.

That all sounded reasonably easy to achieve and like the sort of life that I would be happy with. But as I grew into a young adult, being happy with those typical 'great Australian dream' goals wasn't enough. Becoming financially stable didn't happen overnight, and meeting the love of my life wasn't working for me (I felt like girlfriends just slowed me down). The only thing that was working were my jobs, so I threw all my efforts into that, and improving myself as a person, and figured the rest would fall into line as time went on.

I wasn't always a good kid as a young fella. Actually, I was totally out of control and did quite a few things that let my mum down. And it was seeing that disappointment in my single, hardworking mum that made me change. I wanted to prove to myself, and to Mum, that I could become a better person and a son that a mum could be proud of. I promised her that I would finish school. I didn't graduate with flying colours, that's for sure, but I graduated nonetheless.

When I was 17, I said my goodbyes and hit the road,

leaving South Australia to head north with no plan or idea of what lay ahead. I had quite a few jobs along the way and a lot, and I mean *a lot*, of ups and downs. But I kept pushing through. What I learnt very quickly is that without any trade qualification or tertiary education, I had to invest in myself, upskilling in any way I could, whether that was doing a short course or getting a specialised machinery licence. I also said yes to everything and anything, no matter how crap the work was, because I knew that as long as I was working and trying my hand at new things I was adding new skills, insights and knowledge to my resumé.

At the heart of who I was as a kid and a young adult, and who I am today, is valuing and respecting people. I always make the time to develop and maintain friendships and business relationships because that is what life, love and work is built on. I've also seen that, in life, it is often more a case of who you know, not what you know, so if you maintain integrity and build a solid reputation as an honest, loyal, hardworking person then you will go places.

I was never 'too good for' or 'above' any job, and never said no to an opportunity for work. Even when I had no idea what I was meant to do, I just made sure I worked it out quick-smart. I think that coming from a working-class family and battling at times was a blessing in disguise. I knew that anything is better than having nothing, so I did everything in my power to create a life for me and have something. And the one thing I did have was good groundings and a solid work ethic, instilled in me by my mum, as well as a passion to achieve; to actually *be someone* and *do something* that made a difference in the world.

I see a lot of self-entitled kids these days, and some of them don't get very far because they scrunch their nose up about working at a supermarket checkout, or don't want to have to work hard to prove themselves in a low-paying job before progressing to the next step. I didn't have that luxury, so I was a toilet cleaner, bed-maker, driller, camp host, barman – the list goes on.

I finally felt like I'd achieved something when I saved up enough money to get my chopper licence, which was no walk in the park for someone who isn't book-smart. I was fine practically but the theoretical stuff . . . I don't know how many times I sat and resat some of those units. But the feeling of having a piece of paper with my name on it that enabled me the freedom to fly and do it as a job was one of the best feelings.

•

When I was 23 I worked as a ringer on Moroak Cattle Station, fencing, mustering and cleaning. As any ringer knows, to succeed in that job, you've got to be a jack-of-all-trades.

'Hey, Matty, can you shoe a horse?' my boss asked me one day.

'Yeah, no problem,' I said. 'Mum showed me a few times on the farm when I was younger, so I'll work it out again pretty easy.'

'Righto then, there's thirty horses out the back, bring them in tomorrow morning and start chucking a few shoes on. We've got to muster in a few days.'

Holy shit, I thought to myself, *it's going to take me more than a few days to sort this one out*. So that night I went around the camp asking a few lads about putting shoes on. Everyone was in the same boat as me: they had absolutely no idea. It soon became obvious as to why the boss asked me, because there was no one else. Anyway, I had basic knowledge and called my mum that night, asking her 101 questions. Morning time broke and I was dreading the job, but wasn't going to quit now. I ran the horses in, ready for action with all the gear but no clue.

The first fella was pretty good and quiet – happy for me to lift his feet, cut the shit out and rasp down his long-overgrown nail, bend the shoe into place and nail it on.

Yes! I thought. *That wasn't too hard*. It turned out I had declared victory too soon.

I drafted the next one in, a mare on heat, and she didn't look very happy. Same deal: I secured the halter and started with a nice touch around the feet, trying to lift them one at a time. She had her ears back, trying to nip at me every so often. A little more time passed, and I thought she had calmed down and was at ease. I got the front shoes on with a few jumps and a couple of nips, but all in all she was going well. Time for the back feet. I got her hoof cradled in my crutch and started cleaning the foot out. The next thing I knew I was flying through the air before crumpling into the cattle yards with a massive pain shooting through my mid-section.

'Shit, that hurt,' I said to myself.

I heard a voice from the back of the yard. 'Jesus, are you okay?'

I stood up and brushed myself off. 'How ya going? I'm Matt,' I said to this fella, who I'd never seen before.

'I'm Nolan,' the bloke said, in an American accent. 'I've just got in from Texas. A friend of mine has lined me up with a little work here on the cattle station.'

'You know anything about shoeing horses?' I asked.

'Yeah, that's my main job back home,' he replied.

That's music to my ears, I thought, wanting to do the Toyota jump then and there.

'Any chance you could give me a hand to get through this mob?' I asked. 'We gotta go mustering in a few days and if every horse is the same as this cranky bitch I'm gonna come out of here looking like I've just done 12 rounds with Muhammad Ali.'

'Yes, sir, it would be my pleasure to give you a hand,' he said.

Over the next three days we hooked in and got the rest of the horses done, and over that time I learnt so many new things about what to do and what not to do when you shoe a horse: all the tricks of the trade.

'You've really got the hang of this now, Matt. You'll be teaching everyone else soon,' Nolan said, when we were done.

I was so grateful to him and stoked to have another skill under my belt. I knew it would come in handy again in the future, especially as a ringer. It was sink or swim at the time and a lot of young lads were getting the flick, but I stepped up and got the job done, much to my boss's surprise. But saying yes to that job kept me in a job, and my boss was none the wiser.

After a few more months on the ground, my boss decided to put me in a chopper to start mustering. I was thrilled, but I also knew in the back of my mind, if I ballsed this one up I was gone, and there were 100 pilots sitting on the fence waiting to nick my job. Another old boss of mine once said to me, 'Matt, if you don't fuck up you're not really trying'.

I didn't mind the saying, except I've often felt like I'm cursed. I'm absolutely one of those people that bad stuff always happens to and especially in my twenties it felt like everything I touched would go wrong; it must have been all the karma coming back to bite me in the arse from when I was a kid. But as clichéd as it is, you've got to make mistakes in order to learn from them. There are so many people now that have the ability to achieve great things. But they're too worried about taking a risk or making a mistake that they just coast through life not ever stepping outside of their comfort zone.

After four years of working as a mustering pilot, I started to head home every so often to see my mum and old school friends. Everyone in South Australia was interested in what I'd been up to in northern Australia: flying, drilling and exploring the outback. The more I came home the more I would hear mates say, 'Gee, you're living the dream' or 'You're so lucky with the life you live, someone's really been looking over you'.

It started to get to me. In a way, I *was* lucky that I was able to do what I was passionate about, but what a lot of these people didn't see were the hard yards and sacrifices I had made to get where I was. They just saw me as this footloose and fancy-free cowboy, flying the skies and drinking beers at the pub. What they didn't know about was the months and years on end of working around the clock to make a dollar, or to achieve the next goal.

I used to write in a diary every day, and not long ago I came across all of the diaries I'd kept as a young lad, trying to make something of myself. At the start of each week I had written each one of my expected expenses, along with my weekly income and my savings. Then beneath it I would write my savings goal for the next week: sometimes it was only $50, but that was a lot to me back then.

When I started flying my first wage was $17,500 a year, which never bothered me because I was doing what I loved and was gaining valuable experience along the way. I learnt from everyone that I could, kept my mouth closed and my head down. Life went on, and I gained more insight and, most of all, good relationships. These became my most prized possessions. When you're a young pilot, you love hearing stories of local legend chopper pilots who are the best in the business. Their names were always spoken of as if they were gods – the way they flew, how they could muster some of the toughest cattle and, most of all, never have an accident. As my flying career excelled and I felt myself getting better, I knew I wanted to become one of those pilots, a leader in the field.

I worked for North Australian Helicopters until I was 27. My chief pilot there was John Logan and I remember him saying once, 'Matty, if you make it to 5000 hours without an accident you're good pilot. If you get to 10,000 hours then you're a great pilot. Take it steady and don't kill yourself over a crappy cow that doesn't want to go to the yards. Pick your battles and fly smart.' So, I set my goals to never screw up in a chopper, paying attention to detail at all times and never getting too confident. I've had one flying mishap in Canada, in my early days, but I never damaged the chopper or myself, which is a pretty solid run for nearly 20 years of flying.

•

Starting the filming side of things was one of my biggest challenges. I was still working on cattle stations and everyone there enjoyed having a laugh with me when I pulled out my handy cam. I loved the idea of putting together little fun videos for my family and friends and didn't mind looking like an absolute idiot. I wasn't any good in front of the camera and the blokes on the station would wet themselves laughing calling me 'Hollywood' and making me feel like an absolute twat. But I knew that I could do it. I loved telling stories, and figured it was just a matter of time and that, with practice, it wouldn't take long before I became more natural on camera. I had jackaroos, cooks, girlfriends and pretty much any ring-in I could find to film for me while I was doing my job. I'd save all my footage and then on my days off when everyone went into town to sink piss I'd book a flight to Cairns, hire a cheap hotel room and book an editing suite for the day to start cutting my footage together. At this stage, I was just sending the videos back home to show everyone what I was getting up to up north – mustering, catching wild bulls, fishing, catching crocs and collecting croc eggs. It was so foreign to everyone down south, so they loved what I was putting together. The hardest thing was having to watch myself back and cringing when I saw myself on screen, with my corny one-liners and daggy jokes, but the more I watched it the more I could see how to improve, and I slowly got better.

Imagination, drive and thinking outside the box is key to me and my success. I've never earnt a great deal of money but have always been happy with the path I'm on. When I hit my 30s I still had no real commitments or responsibilities. I continued working hard on investing in myself and always looking for the next challenge. I got to a point where I'd exceeded most of my expectations of what I dreamt of as a kid. I had a chopper licence, had flown around the world working in Canada and owned (well, the bank owned) two small properties. But I still felt like there was more.

I had to work out whether I wanted to pursue my flying career and or follow the TV. I decided to move back to Darwin and see where the TV side of things would take me, giving up a career path I had worked so hard to get. Moving into a small donga out the back of my mate's place, I started chopper tours taking people fishing and on adventures around the Northern Territory. I cross hired a mate's chopper to do the work and used it to film more stuff in an attempt to get traction for a TV show scissor reel.

After lots of empty promises, a stint with the Discovery Channel, a broken contract and a lot of 'no's, 'come back later's, 'maybe next year's, 'you don't have what it takes's and 'you'll never get a show's, I finally got a gig with Nat Geo and *Outback Wrangler* was born. It was no easy feat. I had to sell one of my properties and spent every cent I had on chopper hire and filming. There were a lot of times where I felt like giving up, especially because everything I was investing in and pushing for came out of my back pocket and it was already a very shallow pocket. So at the end of filming I had nothing left in the bank but I had achieved what I set out to do. And following the first episode of *Wrangler*, more doors started to open for me.

More people wanted to come on my tourism trips and I started partnering with different brands and doing TV talk shows. But the more I did, the more the tall poppy syndrome I experienced, and the great (or not so great) Aussie comments continued to roll in again and again: 'You're a lucky bastard', 'You've been kissed on the dick' and 'Who did you screw to get your show?'.

It made my blood boil, because I came from nothing, still had virtually nothing and was trying to have a crack so I could finally be something. I wasn't in Hollywood playing the lead role in *Gladiator*, it was just me doing a little outback show on a doco channel. All the same, I was chuffed to get the gig, especially since I'd been working hard on it for six years and, just as I was about to give up, it all paid off.

With the success of *Outback Wrangler*, even though it wasn't a large personal financial gain, it was a great stepping stone and fantastic profile-building, and with that came a lot more credibility to me and my brand. I thought that with *Wrangler* out there and having a little bit of a profile, tourism was the next best thing to start a stable cash-flow business to tide me over while I pursued filming. I got a great break there. My mate Mick Burns gave me his chopper and said I could pay him back whenever I had a chance. I'd worked with Mick for some time, so he knew I would commit to paying it off.

I was shitting myself because it was a $500,000 machine and the most expensive thing I'd ever bought. I dreaded the idea of crashing it or something happening to it because I didn't want to do anything to compromise our friendship. Every single cent I earnt I put back to Mick. It was $20,000 and $30,000 that I gave him some months and others I'd be left with a couple grand, but I was happy to live in a shed because I knew I was getting ahead.

It took three years to pay off. I had $20,000 left to pay and ironically that same week my last payment was due,

I landed on a reef, the tide came in too quickly and the chopper sank. I actually laughed and laughed at the time, thinking, *Only me, only me would this happen to*. But at that point it didn't matter, because insurance covered it and I was able to pay Mick the last $20,000 and buy myself another chopper outright.

Outback Wrangler slowed for a bit, so I focused on building my tourism business and with that came Outback Floatplane Adventures. This brought a new level of challenges, non-stop work and success of a different kind. Seeing the joy on people's faces and the wildlife not only flourishing but enjoying interacting with humans, thanks to all the work I did out there, was so satisfying. The business grew practically overnight and everyone loved it.

But again people would say 'How lucky are you to do this as a job', 'You call fishing work?' and 'You've got the best job in the world.' Yes, I love my job and consider myself a lucky bloke, but what everyone doesn't see is the behind-the-scenes midnight fuel runs, working on airboats into the early hours of the morning and the logistical nightmares and big expenses involved with managing a lot of staff and machinery. A series of staff stuff-ups cost me a quarter of a million dollars in one month with an airboat engine blowing up, a helicopter over-speeding, and my brand-new land cruiser rolling and crashing. It was hard selling out the company in 2018, but it has left me with a huge sense of success, leaving behind a fantastic tourism product in the Territory.

Today my focus is around MATT WRIGHT, EXPLORE THE WILD, which is my new tourism company offering a number of new and exciting tour products to people in the Territory. And the rest of my time goes to *Outback Wrangler*, which is going from strength to strength both here and overseas. It's paying its own way now and getting better and better with each season. It's been a long journey with its fair share of setbacks and wins, but following my dreams, passions and wild ideas to make a buck has finally got me to where I want to be. Now, at nearly 40, I have a sense of contentment I've never had before, and I can honestly say that my two proudest achievements area making my mum proud and marrying my amazing wife, Kaia. Nothing compares . . .